# English

Assessment Papers

11⁺-12⁺ years

Book 1

# OXFORD
## UNIVERSITY PRESS

Great Clarendon Street, Oxford, OX2 6DP, United Kingdom

Oxford University Press is a department of the University of Oxford. It furthers the University's objective of excellence in research, scholarship, and education by publishing worldwide. Oxford is a registered trade mark of Oxford University Press in the UK and in certain other countries

Text © J M Bond and Sarah Lindsay 2015
Illustrations © Oxford University Press 2015

The moral rights of the authors have been asserted

First published in 2015

All rights reserved. No part of this publication may be reproduced, stored in a retrieval system, or transmitted, in any form or by any means, without the prior permission in writing of Oxford University Press, or as expressly permitted by law, by licence or under terms agreed with the appropriate reprographics rights organization. Enquiries concerning reproduction outside the scope of the above should be sent to the Rights Department, Oxford University Press, at the address above.

You must not circulate this work in any other form and you must impose this same condition on any acquirer

British Library Cataloguing in Publication Data
Data available

978-0-19-274007-6

10 9 8 7

Paper used in the production of this book is a natural, recyclable product made from wood grown in sustainable forests. The manufacturing process conforms to the environmental regulations of the country of origin.

Printed in China

**Acknowledgements**

The publishers would like to thank the following for permissions to use copyright material:

Page make-up: GreenGate Publishing Services, Tonbridge, Kent
Illustrations: Nigel Kitching
Cover illustrations: Lo Cole

Extract from *Cider with Rosie* by Laurie Lee, published by Hogarth Press. Reprinted by permission of The Random House Group Ltd; extract from *Jonathan Livingston Seagull: A Story* by Richard Bach, reprinted by permission of HarperCollins Publishers Ltd; extract from *The River Cottage Cookbook* by Hugh Fearnley-Whittingstall, reprinted by permission of HarperCollins Publishers Ltd; extract from *The Highwayman* by Alfred Noyes, reprinted by permission of The Society of Authors as the Literary Representative of the estate of Alfred Noyes; extract from Times Online *A Dahl of a day out* by Damian Kelleher / NI Syndication Ltd, 2006; extract from *A Small Pinch of Weather* 'The Cost of Night' by Joan Aiken, reprinted by permission of Lutterworth Press.

Although we have made every effort to trace and contact all copyright holders before publication this has not been possible in all cases. If notified, the publisher will rectify any errors or omissions at the earliest opportunity.

Links to third party websites are provided by Oxford in good faith and for information only. Oxford disclaims any responsibility for the materials contained in any third party website referenced in this work.

# Before you get started

## What is Bond?

This book is part of the Bond Assessment Papers series for English, which provides **thorough and continuous practice of key English skills** from ages five to thirteen. Bond's English resources are ideal preparation for many different kinds of tests and exams – from SATs to 11+ and other secondary school selection exams.

## How does the scope of this book match real exam content?

*English 11+-12+ Book 1* and *Book 2* are the advanced Bond 11+ books. Each paper is **pitched a level above a typical 11+ exam**, providing greater challenge and stretching skills further. The papers practise comprehension, spelling, grammar and vocabulary work. They are also in line with other selective exams for this age group. The coverage supports the National Curriculum and the National Literacy Strategy and will also **provide invaluable preparation for higher level Key Stage 2 SATs performance**. It is outside the scope of this book to practise extended and creative writing skills. *Bond Focus on Writing* provides full coverage of writing skills.

## What does the book contain?

- **10 papers** – each one contains 100 questions.
- **Tutorial links throughout** – 📖 – this icon appears in the margin next to the questions. It indicates links to the relevant section in *How to do 11+ English*, our invaluable subject guide that offers explanations and practice for all core question types.
- **Scoring devices** – there are score boxes in the margins and a Progress Chart on page 64. The chart is a visual and motivating way for children to see how they are doing. It also turns the score into a percentage that can help decide what to do next.
- **Next Step Planner** – advice on what to do after finishing the papers can be found on the inside back cover.
- **Answers** – located in an easily-removed central pull-out section.

## How can you use this book?

One of the great strengths of Bond Assessment Papers is their flexibility. They can be used at home, in school and by tutors to:

- set **timed formal practice tests** – allow about 50 minutes per paper in line with standard 11+ demands. Reduce the suggested time limit by five minutes to practise working at speed.

- provide **bite-sized chunks** for regular practice
- **highlight strengths and weaknesses** in the core skills
- identify **individual needs**
- set **homework**
- follow a **complete 11+ preparation strategy** alongside *The Parents' Guide to the 11+* (see below).

It is best to start at the beginning and work though the papers in order. If you are using the book as part of a careful run in to the 11+, we suggest that you also have four other essential Bond resources close at hand:

*How to do 11+ English*: the subject guide that explains all the question types practised in this book. Use the cross-reference icons to find the relevant sections.

*Focus on Comprehension*: the practical handbook that clearly shows children how to read and understand the text, understand the questions and assess their own answers.

*Focus on Writing*: the essential resource that explains the key components of successful writing.

*The Parents' Guide to the 11+*: the step-by-step guide to the whole 11+ experience. It clearly explains the 11+ process, provides guidance on how to assess children, helps you to set complete action plans for practice and explains how you can use *English 11+-12+ Book 1* and *Book 2* as part of a strategic run-in to the exam.

See the inside front cover for more details of these books.

## What does a score mean and how can it be improved?

It is unfortunately impossible to guarantee that a child will pass the 11+ exam if they achieve a certain score on any practice book or paper. Success on the day depends on a host of factors, including the scores of the other children sitting the test. However, we can give some guidance on what a score indicates and how to improve it.

If children colour in the Progress Chart on page 64, this will give an idea of present performance in percentage terms. The Next Step Planner inside the back cover will help you to decide what to do next to help a child progress. It is always valuable to go over wrong answers with children. If they are having trouble with any particular question type, follow the tutorial links to *How to do 11+ English* for step-by-step explanations and further practice.

## Don't forget the website…!

Visit www.bond11plus.co.uk for lots of advice, information and suggestions on everything to do with Bond, the 11+ and helping children to do their best.

# Key words

Some special words are used in this book. You will find them in **bold** each time they appear in the Papers. These words are explained here.

| | |
|---|---|
| **abbreviation** | a word or words which is/are shortened |
| **active verb** | when the main person or thing does the action   he <u>took</u> it |
| **adjective** | a word that describes somebody or something |
| **adjectival phrase** | a group of words describing a noun |
| **adverb** | a word that gives extra meaning to a verb |
| **alphabetical order** | words arranged in the order found in the alphabet |
| **antonym** | a word with a meaning opposite to another word   hot – cold |
| **clause** | a section of a sentence with a verb |
| **collective noun** | a word referring to a group   swarm |
| **compound word** | a word made up of two other words   football |
| **conditional** | a clause or sentence expressing the idea that one thing depends on something else |
| **conjunction** | a word used to link sentences, phrases or words   and, but |
| **connective** | a word or words that joins clauses or sentences |
| **contraction** | two words shortened into one with an apostrophe placed where the letter/s have been dropped   do not = don't |
| **definition** | a meaning of a word |
| **diminutive** | a word implying smallness   booklet |
| **homophone** | a word that has the same sound as another but a different meaning or spelling   right/write |
| **infinitive** | the base form of a verb without any additional endings   clap |
| **metaphor** | an expression in which something is described in terms usually associated with another   the sky is a <u>sapphire</u> sea |
| **mnemonic** | a device to learn particular spellings   There is <u>a rat</u> in sep<u>a</u>r<u>at</u>e |
| **modal verb** | used to help other words explain when something is necessary or possible   I <u>can</u> do my homework easily |
| **noun** | a word for somebody or something |
| **onomatopoeic** | a word that echoes a sound, associated with its meaning   hiss |
| **passive verb** | when the main person or thing has the action done to it   <u>it was taken by him</u> |
| **past tense** | form of a verb showing that something has already happened |
| **phrase** | a group of words that act as a unit |
| **plural** | more than one   cats |
| **prefix** | a group of letters added to the beginning of a word   un, dis |
| **preposition** | a word that relates other words to each other   the book <u>on</u> the table |
| **pronoun** | a word used to replace a noun   them |
| **root word** | a word to which prefixes or suffixes can be added to make other words   <u>quick</u>ly |
| **sentence** | a unit of written language which makes sense by itself |
| **simile** | an expression to describe what something is like   as cold as ice |
| **singular** | one   cat |
| **suffix** | a group of letters added to the end of a word   ly, ful |
| **superlative** | describes the limit of a quality (adjective or adverb)   most/least or shortest |
| **synonym** | a word with the same or very similar meaning as another word   quick – fast |
| **verb** | a 'doing' or 'being' word |

# Paper 1

*The author, Laurie Lee, wrote this book about his childhood memories.*

The frozen pond on such a winter's evening was a very treadmill of pleasure. Time was uncounted; we played ourselves into exhaustion. We ran and slid till we dripped with sweat; our scarves were pearled with our breath. The reeds and horse-tails at the pond's edge smelt as pungent as old men's fingers. Hanging branches of willow, manacled in the ice, bloomed like lilac in the setting sun. Then the frost moon rose through the charcoal trees and we knew that we'd played too long.

   We had promised Mother we would fetch some wood. We had to get some each day in winter. Jack and I, hands in pockets, mooched silently up the lane; it was night now, and we were frightened. The beech wood was a cavern of moonlight and shadows, and we kept very close together.

   The dead sticks on the ground were easily seen, glittering with the night's new frost. As we ripped them from the earth, scabbed with soil and leaves, our hands began to burn with the cold. The wood was silent and freezing hard, white and smelling of wolves. Such a night as lost hunters must have stared upon when first they wandered north into the Ice Age. We thought of caves, warm skins and fires, grabbed our sticks, and tore off home.

   Then there were 'Where've-you-beens?', 'Never-minds', 'Oh-Dears', and 'Come-by-the-fire-you-look-half-dead'. First the long slow torment as our hands thawed out, a quiet agony of returning blood. Worse than toothache it was; I sat there sobbing, but gradually the pain wave passed. Then we had jugs of tea, hot toast and dripping; and later our sisters came. 'It was murder in Stroud. I fell down twice – in the High Street – and tore my stockings. I'm sure I showed everything. It was terrible, Ma. And a horse went through Maypole's window. And old Mr Fowler couldn't get down the hill and had to sit on his bottom and slide. It's freezing harder than ever now. We won't none of us be able to budge tomorrow.'

They sat at their tea and went on talking about it in their sing-song disaster voices. And we boys were content to know the winter had come, total winter, the new occupation... .

Later, towards Christmas, there was heavy snow, which raised the roads to the tops of the hedges. There were millions of tons of the lovely stuff, plastic, pure, all-purpose, which nobody owned, which one could carve or tunnel, eat, or just throw about. It covered the hills and cut off the villages, but nobody thought of rescues; for there was hay in the barns and flour in the kitchens, the women baked bread, the cattle were fed and sheltered – we'd been cut off before, after all.

The week before Christmas, when the snow seemed to lie thickest, was the moment for carol-singing; and when I think back to those nights it is to the crunch of snow and to the lights of the lanterns on it. Carol-singing in my village was a special tithe for the boys; the girls had little to do with it. Like hay-making, blackberrying, stone-clearing, and wishing-people-a-happy-Easter, it was one of our seasonal perks.

By instinct we knew just when to begin it; a day too soon and we should have been unwelcome, a day too late and we should have received lean looks from people whose bounty was already exhausted. When the true moment came, exactly balanced, we recognised it and were ready.

So as soon as the wood had been stacked in the oven to dry for the morning fire, we put on our scarves and went out through the streets, calling loudly between our hands, till the various boys who knew the signal ran out from their houses to join us.

One by one they came stumbling over the snow, swinging their lanterns around their heads, shouting and coughing horribly.

'Coming carol-barking then?'

We were the Church Choir, so no answer was necessary. For a year we had praised the Lord out of key, and as a reward for this service – on top of the Outing – we now had the right to visit all the big houses, to sing our carols and collect our tribute.

To work them all meant a five-mile foot journey over wild and generally snowed-up country. So the first thing we did was to plan our route; a formality, as the route never changed. All the same, we blew on our fingers and argued; and then we chose our Leader. This was not binding, for we all fancied ourselves as Leaders, and he who started the night in that position usually trailed home with a bloody nose.

From *Cider with Rosie* by Laurie Lee

Answer these questions.

1  How did Laurie know he had played too long?

---

2  What relation is Jack to the writer?

---

**3–5** Find three pieces of evidence from the passage that convey to the reader how cold it is on this winter's evening.

_____

_____

_____

**6–7** Explain why the thawing of Laurie's hands is described as a 'long slow torment' (line 18).

_____

_____

_____

**8–9** Using evidence from the passage, describe Laurie's mother.

_____

_____

_____

**10** Which town did Laurie live near? _____

**11–12** Why are Laurie's sisters described as having 'sing-song disaster voices' (line 26)?

_____

_____

**13** What evidence is there in the passage that indicates Laurie's love of the snow?

_____

**14** A tithe was a tax. What do you think it means in this passage (line 38)?

_____

**15** Why, on line 39, are the activities listed seen as 'seasonal perks'?

_____

**16** Which word, in the paragraphs describing the carol singing, means generosity?

_____

**17** Why does Laurie describe the faces of people as having 'lean looks' if they arrived a day too late (line 41)?

_____

**18** What does 'instinct' mean (line 40)?

_____

**19–20** Which two **phrases** in the passage suggest the Church Choir wasn't very good?

_____

_____

Form a **noun** from each of the **verbs** in bold.

**21 provide**    They bought the _____ at the supermarket.

**22 enter**      They couldn't find the _____ to the caves.

**23 choose**     They had the _____ of going to the seaside or to a farm.

**24 advertise**  The _____ said that the concert started at 7.30 p.m.

**25 perform**    The _____ of the school play was excellent.

**26 bewilder**   The child's _____ was plain to see.

**27 destroy**    The army was responsible for the _____ of the bridge.

**28 applaud**    The _____ was deafening.

Fill in the missing letter in each word with an *a*, *e* or *o*.

**29** decorat___r       **30** cell___r         **31** plumb___r

**32** disast___r        **33** corrid___r       **34** burgl___r

**35** popul___r         **36** circul___r       **37** divis___r

**38** direct___r        **39** propriet___r     **40** partn___r

Write the following using indirect speech.

**41–45** Dad said, "I am going to mow the lawn. I hope this is the last time I will have to do it this year as I am tired of doing it."

Dad said that _____ going to mow the lawn.

_____ this _____ the last time _____ have to do it this year as _____ tired of doing it.

Write *there*, *their* or *they're* in each gap.

46–47 _____ going to dive into the pool when _____ teacher blows the whistle.

48–49 Where are _____ coats? _____ soaking!

50–51 _____ is no point hiding the chocolate box _____!

52–53 _____ is a strong wind which has blown some tiles off _____ roof.

Write the **contraction** for each of these.

54  they have  _____

55  I would  _____

56  will not  _____

In each space, write the word class of the underlined word.

57  Close the back door.  _____

58  We said we would back Hotspot to win the race.  _____

59  Dad's got a pain in his back.  _____

60  Come back soon.  _____

Write three **compound words** using each of the words listed.

61–63  light  _____  _____  _____

64–66  snow  _____  _____  _____

67–69  day  _____  _____  _____

Underline the unstressed vowels in each word.

70  postage          71  sentence          72  parliament

73  machinery     74  fattening          75  mathematics

76  history

Rewrite these **sentences** changing them from **singular** to **plural**.

77–80  The man was cleaning his house.

_____

**81–82** She jumped over the puddle.

**83–86** He bought a scarf to support his football team.

Underline the correct **homophone** in each sentence.

**87** The (principle/principal) message of the speech was that we all need to work together.

**88** The midfielder (past, passed) the ball to the striker, who scored a goal.

**89** We (rode, rowed) our bikes along the canal path until it became dark.

**90** Do you know (who's, whose) car is blocking the drive?

**91** My parents insist that we recycle whatever we can because they hate to (waste, waist) anything.

**92** We followed the signs for the holiday (root, route) along the motorway.

**93** I always turn away when I'm watching a nature programme that shows a lion catching its (prey, pray).

**94** 'Hurry or we are going (to, too) be late!'

**95** The training (coarse, course) began at 9:00 in the morning.

Rewrite the passage adding the missing commas.

**96–100** Sam was caught thank goodness otherwise I would have been blamed for stealing the sweets pen magazine Harry Potter book and racing car.

# Paper 2

It wasn't long before Jonathan Gull was off by himself again, far out to sea, hungry, happy, learning.

The subject was speed, and in a week's practice he learned more about speed than the fastest gull alive.

From a thousand feet, flapping his wings as hard as he could, he pushed over into a blazing steep dive towards the waves, and learned why seagulls don't make blazing steep power-dives. In just six seconds he was moving seventy miles per hour, the speed at which one's wing goes unstable on the upstroke.

Time after time it happened. Careful as he was, working at the very peak of his ability, he lost control at high speed.

Climb to a thousand feet. Full power straight ahead first, then push over, flapping, to a vertical dive. Then, every time, his left wing stalled on an upstroke, he'd roll violently left, stall his right wing recovering, and flick like fire into a wild tumbling spin to the right.

He couldn't be careful enough on that upstroke. Ten times he tried, and all ten times, as he passed through seventy miles per hour, he burst into a churning mass of feathers, out of control, crashing down into the water.

The key, he thought at last, dripping wet, must be to hold the wings still at high speeds – to flap up to fifty and then hold the wings still.

From two thousand feet he tried again, rolling into his dive, beak straight down, wings full out and stable from the moment he passed fifty miles per hour. It took tremendous strength, but it worked. In ten seconds he had blurred through ninety miles per hour. Jonathan had set a world speed record for seagulls!

But victory was short-lived. The instant he began his pullout, the instant he changed the angle of his wings, he snapped into the same terrible uncontrolled disaster, and at ninety miles per hour it hit him like dynamite. Jonathan Seagull exploded in midair and smashed down into a brick-hard sea.

When he came to, it was well after dark, and he floated in moonlight on the surface of the ocean. His wings were ragged bars of lead, but the weight of failure was even heavier on his back. He wished, feebly, that the weight could be just enough to drag him gently down to the bottom, and end it all.

As he sank low in the water, a strange hollow voice sounded within him. There's no way around it. I am a seagull. I am limited by my nature. If I were meant to learn so much about flying, I'd have charts for brains. If I were meant to fly at speed, I'd have a falcon's short wings, and live on mice instead of fish. My father was right. I must forget this foolishness. I must fly home to the Flock and be content as I am, as a poor limited seagull.

The voice faded, and Jonathan agreed. The place for a seagull at night is on shore, and from this moment forth, he vowed, he would be a normal gull. It would make everyone happier.

He pushed wearily away from the dark water and flew towards the land, grateful for what he had learned about work-saving low-altitude flying.

But no, he thought. I am done with the way I was, I am done with everything I learned. I am a seagull like every other seagull, and I will fly like one. So he climbed painfully to a hundred feet and flapped his wings harder, pressing for shore.

He felt better for his decision to be just another one of the flock. There would be no ties now to the force that had driven him to learn, there would be no more challenge and no more failure. And it was pretty, just to stop thinking, and fly through the dark, toward the lights above the beach.

*Dark!* The hollow voice cracked in alarm. *Seagulls never fly in the dark!*

Jonathan was not alert to listen. It's pretty, he thought. The moon and the lights twinkling on the water, throwing out little beacon-trails through the night, and all so peaceful and still … .

Get down! Seagulls never fly in the dark! If you were meant to fly in the dark, you'd have the eyes of an owl! You'd have charts for brains! You'd have a falcon's short wings!

There in the night, a hundred feet in the air, Jonathan Livingston Seagull blinked. His pain, his resolutions, vanished.

Short wings. *A falcon's short wings!*

That's the answer! What a fool I've been! All I need is a tiny little wing, all I need is to fold most of my wings and fly on just the tips alone! *Short wings!*

He climbed two thousand feet above the black sea, and without a moment for thought of failure and death, he brought his forewings tightly in to his body, left only the narrow swept daggers of his wingtips extended into the wind, and fell into a vertical dive.

The wind was a monster roar at his head. Seventy miles per hour, ninety, a hundred and twenty and faster still. The wing-strain now at a hundred and forty miles per hour wasn't nearly as hard as it had been before at seventy, and with the faintest twist of his wingtips he eased out of the dive and shot above the waves, a grey cannonball under the moon.

He closed his eyes to slits against the wind and rejoiced. A hundred and forty miles per hour! And under control! If I dive from five thousand feet instead of two thousand, I wonder how fast ..?

His vows of a moment before were forgotten, swept away in that great swift wind. Yet he felt guiltless, breaking the promises he had made himself. Such promises are only for the gulls that accept the ordinary. One who has touched excellence in his learning has no need of that kind of promise.

From *Jonathan Livingston Seagull: A Story* by Richard Bach

Answer these questions.

1 At what speed did Jonathan stall each time?

2 Which wing caused Jonathan to stall?

3 From what height did Jonathan first break the world speed record for seagulls?

4 Write a **synonym** for the word 'tremendous' (line 22). _____

5 What hit Jonathan like 'dynamite' (line 26)?

_____

6 Why, on line 27, was the sea described as 'brick-hard'?

_____

7–8 Find two pieces of evidence in the passage that show how desperate Jonathan felt having crashed at ninety miles per hour.

_____

_____

9 What does 'from this moment forth' (line 39) mean?

_____

10 Which bird is mentioned in the passage as having short wings? _____

11 Which **phrase** conveys Jonathan's true feelings about being a gull?

_____

12–13 Why was Jonathan 'not alert to listen' on line 51? Use evidence from the passage to support your answer.

_____

_____

14 Give one reason why gulls never fly in the dark.

_____

15 Why did Jonathan blink in line 58?

_____

16–17 Jonathan is described as 'a grey cannonball' on line 70. Explain why this **phrase** is used.

_____

_____

18–20 Look at the final paragraph again. Describe the key characteristics of Jonathan Livingston Seagull.

_____

_____

_____

20

Give the **plurals** of the following **nouns**.

21  mouse  _____     22  story  _____

23  cargo/cargoes  _____     24  thief  _____

25  trolley  _____     26  potato  _____

27  gas  _____     28  ox  _____

29  roof  _____     30  valley  _____

Match the words with their **definitions**. Write the correct number in the space.

31  conservation  _____     (1) secret

32  constellation  _____     (2) assembly

33  conversation  _____     (3) informal discussion

34  confidential  _____     (4) group of stars

35  consecutive  _____     (5) one after the other, in order

36  congregation  _____     (6) preservation

Put the words in bold in their correct places so the extract below makes sense.

37–46    **movement    wedge    cook    ashore    crutch**
         **deck    walk    spaces    lanyard    heaviest**

Long John Silver, our ship's _____ – Barbecue as the men called him – carried his _____ by a _____ round his neck, to have both hands as free as possible. It was something to see him _____ the foot of his crutch against a bulkhead, and, propped against it, yielding to every _____ of the ship, get on with his cooking like someone safe _____. Still more strange was it to see him in the _____ of weather, cross the _____. He had a line or two rigged up to help him across the widest _____ and he would hand himself from one place to another as quickly as another man could _____.

From *Treasure Island* by R L Stevenson

Complete the following **similes** using the words in the box.

|  two peas  |  pie  |  hatter  |  cucumber  |
|  lead  |  bat  |  cricket  |  gold  |

47  as alike as  _____      48  as blind as a  _____

49  as cool as a  _____     50  as easy as  _____

51  as good as  _____       52  as heavy as  _____

53  as lively as a  _____   54  as mad as a  _____

Underline the **verbs** in the **sentences**.

55  Ian had a large appetite.
56  Rachel wrote the invitations to her party neatly.
57  She intently watched the TV programme.
58  Softly she sang the lilting tune.
59  They got up early on Sunday.
60–61  He lifted the kitten carefully and put it in the basket.

Write an **antonym** for each of these words.

62  contract   _____      63  import     _____

64  increase   _____      65  fine       _____

66  captive    _____      67  temporary  _____

Write four sentences, each with a **modal verb**.

68  _____

69  _____

70  _____

71  _____

Fill the gap by writing the **past tense** of the word in bold.

72 **creep**     They _____ slowly towards her.

73 **lose**     He _____ his ball when he was out in the woods.

74 **speak**     The lady _____ kindly to the little girl.

75 **ring**     The policewoman _____ the doorbell.

76 **break**     Mum was cross when they _____ the plate.

Circle the **pronouns** in the short passage.

77–83 They jumped into the car before it sped off at high speed. Joseph whispered that his mum had never been so cross. She reminded him of a bull! They agreed with him.

Copy and add the missing punctuation to the following:

84–88 What about the horse You don't mention sending that back said Thorin

_____

_____

_____

Write three words using each of the **prefixes**.

89–91 **dis-**     _____     _____     _____

92–94 **mis-**     _____     _____     _____

Identify what part of speech each of the words in bold are.

The **terrified** **people** **reacted** **badly** when they **were** asked to go in **another** direction.

95 _____     96 _____     97 _____

98 _____     99 _____     100 _____

*Now go to the Progress Chart to record your score!*     Total

# Paper 3

## Snake

A snake came to my water-trough
On a hot, hot day, and I in pyjamas for the heat,
To drink there.

In the deep, strange-scented shade of the great dark carob-tree
I came down the steps with my pitcher 5
And must wait, must stand and wait, for there he was at the trough before me.

He reached down from a fissure in the earth-wall in the gloom
And trailed his yellow-brown slackness soft-bellied down, over the edge of the stone trough
And rested his throat upon the stone bottom,
And where the water had dripped from the tap, in a small clearness, 10
He sipped with his straight mouth,
Softly drank through his straight gums, into his slack long body,
Silently.

Someone was before me at my water-trough,
And I, like a second comer, waiting. 15

He lifted his head from his drinking, as cattle do,
And looked at me vaguely, as drinking cattle do,

And flickered his two-forked tongue from his lips, and mused a moment,
And stooped and drank a little more,
Being earth-brown, earth-golden from the burning bowels of the earth 20
On the day of Sicilian July, with Etna smoking.

The voice of my education said to me
He must be killed,
For in Sicily the black, black snakes are innocent, the gold are venomous.

And voices in me said, *If you were a man* 25
*You would take a stick and break him now, and finish him off*.

But must I confess how I liked him,
How glad I was he had come like a guest in quiet, to drink at my water-trough
And depart peaceful, pacified, and thankless,
Into the burning bowels of this earth? 30

Was it cowardice, that I dared not kill him?
Was it perversity, that I longed to talk to him?
Was it humility, to feel so honoured?
I felt so honoured.

And yet those voices: 35
*If you were not afraid, you would kill him!*

And truly I was afraid, I was most afraid,
But even so, honoured still more
That he should seek my hospitality
From out the dark door of the secret earth. 40

He drank enough
And lifted his head, dreamily, as one who has drunken,
And flickered his tongue like a forked night on the air, so black,
Seeming to lick his lips,
And looked around like a god, unseeing, into the air, 45
And slowly turned his head.

And slowly, very slowly, as if thrice adream,
Proceeded to draw his slow length curving round
And climb again the broken bank of my wall-face …

… I looked round, I put down my pitcher, 50
I picked up a clumsy log
And threw it at the water-trough with a clatter.

I think it did not hit him,
But suddenly that part of him that was left behind convulsed in undignified haste,
Writhing like lightning, and was gone 55
Into the black hole, the earth-lipped fissure in the wall-front,
At which, in the intense still noon, I stared with fascination.

And immediately I regretted it.
I thought how paltry, how vulgar, what a mean act!
I despised myself and the voices of my accursed human education. 60
And I thought of the albatross,
And I wished he would come back, my snake …

by D H Lawrence

Answer these questions.

1 What was at the water-trough when the writer arrived? _____

2 Which **adjective** does the poet use to describe the snake's mouth?

_____

3 In lines 16–17 the snake was compared to cattle. How?

_____

_____

4 Did this scene take place during the day or at night?

_____

**5–7** Give the meaning of the following words as they are used in the poem:

'mused' (line 18) _____

'venomous' (line 24) _____

'perversity' (line 32) _____

**8** Copy a line from the poem that indicates in which country the scene is based.

_____

**9** Find a line or **phrase** that is characteristically used to describe a snake.

_____

**10** Line 34 reads 'I felt so honoured'. Why did the onlooker feel like this?

_____

**11** Why does the poet describe the earth as 'secret' (line 40)?

_____

**12–13** Look again at lines 31–40. Using lines from the poem to support your answer, describe how the onlooker is feeling.

_____

_____

_____

**14–15** What is the snake's attitude while at the drinking trough? Use a line from the poem to support your answer.

_____

_____

**16** The onlooker picked up 'a clumsy log' (line 51). Why was the log described as 'clumsy'?

_____

**17** Using evidence from the poem, explain why the onlooker threw a log at the snake.

_____

_____

_____

**18–19** Describe the physical environment of where the poem is taking place. Use an example from the passage to support your answer.

_____

_____

_____

**20** What is the main point made in the final verse of the poem?

_____

_____

Underline the words below which are of common gender.

**21–27**
| actress | athlete | student | widow |
| policeman | friend | dustman | typist |
| knitter | bride | bachelor | mother |
| girl | child | cat | businessman |

Write the following **abbreviations** in full.

**28** NE _____

**29** PLC _____

**30** PTO _____

**31** Dept _____

**32** mg _____

**33** BST _____

**34** UK _____

Complete each expression with a **preposition**.

**Example** *off* the cuff

**35** _____ the most part

**36** _____ the long run

**37** _____ all fours

**38** _____ the other hand

**39** _____ better or worse

**40** _____ his wits' end

**41** _____ all means

**42** _____ to the hilt

Complete the following words with *ie* or *ei*.

43  for____gn       44  bel____ve       45  ach____ve

46  conc____ted    47  n____ghbour    48  aud____nce

49  h____ght        50  c____ling

On each line, underline the word which is the same part of speech as the word in bold.

| 51 **often** | noble | beautiful | sick | badly | wanting |
| 52 **breathe** | quickly | goat | it | for | slither |
| 53 **height** | quantity | sit | idle | lazy | comfortable |
| 54 **difficult** | soften | woollen | they | worm | grew |
| 55 **why** | time | place | where | town | hour |
| 56 **sad** | dress | bonnet | ship | picture | ugly |
| 57 **and** | sand | boat | badly | but | cut |

Write two words that use the **root word** in bold.

58–59  **help**    _____    _____

60–61  **turn**    _____    _____

62–63  **collect**  _____    _____

Write a formal equivalent for each of these words or phrases.

64  ask         _____       65  go in to    _____

66  find out    _____       67  annoyance   _____

Underline any of these words which should always start with a capital letter.

68–76   envelope   egyptian   film       david      february
        wales      food       function   denmark    nation
        month      june       manchester ornament   tuesday
        queen      kite       britney    log        lion

Spell these words correctly.

77  Febuary     _____       78  tomorow     _____

79  posess      _____       80  goverment   _____

18

Make **nouns** from the words in bold to complete the **sentences**.

81 **punish**   I do not believe in capital _____.

82 **fragrant**   The _____ of the rose was beautiful.

83 **arrive**   The _____ of the pop star at the airport was delayed.

84 **long**   Sarah said that her trousers were not the right _____.

85 **conclude**   At the _____ of the concert we rushed to get home.

86 **assist**   Dad asked Najib for his _____.

Rewrite these **sentences** so they contain only single negatives.

87 Gina didn't swim in no sea.

_____

88 There weren't no stars out tonight.

_____

89 The dogs didn't not wait.

_____

90 The playground wasn't not open.

_____

91 Caroline didn't want no ride in the car.

_____

92 Raj's family hadn't won no money on the lottery.

_____

Write eight **contractions** using the words in bold.

   **are**    **you**    **have**    **will**    **they**    **not**

93–100 _____  _____  _____  _____

   _____  _____  _____  _____

# Paper 4

### Why grow vegetables?

What can I say to the enthusiastic cook who is vaguely interested in the idea of growing his or her own vegetables but is still teetering on the brink of action? Realistically, for most of us these days there are no persuasive economic arguments for growing your own vegetables – at least, not if you cost out your time. (During summer gluts, my father used to pay me pocket money to pick and freeze peas, beans and soft fruits from his vegetable garden. He once calculated that the resulting frozen produce cost him three or four times what it would in the supermarket. And that was without factoring in his own time.)

   But there is still an important sense in which the vegetables you grow yourself really are free. When your time is given freely, what you make with it is free in the best sense of the word. When you buy your vegetables, you are a slave – to the car that takes you to the shops; to the methods, good and bad, by which the vegetables are produced; to the market forces, and the big bosses who fix the prices; to the shelf-stacking policies that determine the freshness, or otherwise, of the produce you buy. You have no say whatsoever in the means of production, no role in the quality of what becomes yours only when you hand over the cash.

   Grow your own vegetables and all that changes. Choose the seeds, the growing site, the time to plant, to weed, to water, to feed, to harvest. What you then take to the kitchen is not just a vegetable, it's a form of self-expression, an assertion of personal liberty. It's a kind of opting out of the world as you're told it must be in favour of the world as you'd like it to be. You may doubt the wisdom of loading something as ordinary as a carrot with such deep personal meaning. But try growing them yourself, and you will find that carrots are far from ordinary. They are sleek, pointed, orange miracles that come from nowhere to populate a bare patch of earth. And, almost astonishingly, you can eat them!

   The fact is, those who already grow their own vegetables for the kitchen need no converting to the cause. I have yet to meet a vegetable gardener who complained that 'it's hardly worth it, what with the choice available in the supermarket these days', or 'it's too much time for too little reward', or 'what's the point, you can hardly taste the difference anyway?' These quotations are the clichés of the uninitiated – those who do not yet know the prickly heat of a fat radish freshly drawn from the earth, washed with a quick wipe on a dewy tuft of grass, then eaten without further ado; those who have not tasted the extra sugar dose in a pile of self-podded peas thrown into boiling water within an hour of being picked; those who have not marvelled at the unrepentant earthiness of freshly dug potatoes …

If you are still wavering, let me offer you another, almost glib answer to the question, 'why grow vegetables?' Because you can. I mean, anyone can. As I said earlier, growing vegetables is easy. All you need is earth and seeds. Sunshine and water are important too, but in a reasonable year both should come in plentiful supply, courtesy of the man upstairs. A relaxed, *laissez-faire* attitude to growing vegetables will stand the beginner in good stead. While there is plenty of scope for fussing and fretting about your vegetable patch, you will probably find that obsessional attention to detail either does or doesn't evolve as the years go by, according to your personality. In other words, if you want to become the manic overseer of a manicured vegetable plot, you can; but it doesn't have to start off that way.

## Starting a vegetable garden

Some thought is required in choosing your patch of ground. All gardeners have to compromise, and while a south-facing, level piece of land, sheltered from the worst of the wind, with a rich, finely textured soil will get you off to a flying start, few of us are blessed with such perfect growing conditions. It's more a question of avoiding negative factors. Light is vital, and a patch that is in near-permanent shade is simply not going to work. It's important, therefore, to be aware of the passage of the sun across your intended growing site from dawn till dusk. If the ground enjoys direct sunlight for more than half of daylight hours (that's about four in mid-winter, eight on the longest day), you should be able to grow well on it. It's worth bearing in mind that you may be able to gain extra sunlight for your patch by cutting down an unfortunately located tree or two. This takes a bit of courage, and there's no point in breaking your heart by sacrificing a beloved feature of your garden for an extra row of peas. But trees are not sacred just because they are big. And of course there's the firewood bonus.

As far as the timing of your bed-creation scheme goes, you have two choices: late autumn for planting the following spring, or early spring for almost immediate planting. An autumn digging will give the soil a chance to settle and leaves time for existing green matter, such as grass tufts and the usual weeds, to rot down. The winter months ahead will allow this to happen without too many new weeds springing up. However, you will have to be on your toes come spring, as the weed seeds in the ground will leap at the first chance they get to germinate and take hold. Another good going over in early March will be essential if you don't want to be back to square one. If you're opting for spring digging, you may as well wait until it's almost time to start planting: say early April. Dig over your patch, removing all the grass and weeds you can, and simply work over your soil till it is nicely broken up and ready for planting.

From *The River Cottage Cookbook* by Hugh Fearnley-Whittingstall

Answer these questions.

1 What did the author's father used to pay him to do?
_____

2 What is meant by 'teetering on the brink of action' (line 3)?
_____

3–5 List and explain three reasons why the author suggests it is not good to buy vegetables.
_____
_____
_____

6 Which vegetable does the author use to inspire vegetable growers?
_____

7 Who needs no converting to the vegetable-growing cause?
_____

8 Does the author believe growing vegetables is easy or hard? _____

9–11 Which four key things do you need to grow vegetables? Explain why.
_____
_____
_____
_____

12 Describe what is meant by a 'laissez-faire attitude' on line 41.
_____

13 What is the meaning of the word 'compromise' (line 50) in this context?
_____

14 Why has the author described the trees as 'unfortunately located' (line 59)?
_____
_____
_____

**15–17** Find three examples from the passage conveying the author's passion for growing vegetables.

_____

_____

_____

**18–20** The next subtitle in the author's book is 'Preparing for sowing'. Write three things the author might cover under this heading.

_____

_____

_____

Write three **onomatopoeic** words that describe sounds made by the following:

**21–23** an engine   _____   _____   _____

**24–26** the wind    _____   _____   _____

Write four *ough* words. The *ough* sound in each word must be different.

27 _____        28 _____

29 _____        30 _____

Add a different **suffix** to each of these **root words**. Rewrite the words correctly.

31 experiment _____     32 prefer _____

33 excite _____         34 thought _____

35 defer _____          36 marry _____

37 excel _____          38 bore _____

Rewrite the **phrases** below in more formal English.

39 See ya later.

_____

40 You're taking the mickey!

_____

23

41 Did you wag school?

_____

42 It was an awesome gig.

_____

43 You look cool in those sunglasses.

_____

Add the missing colons.

44 The following children are absent today Amina, Ilesh, Frank, Michael and Fayza.

45 The school magazine reported No school uniform for a day!

46 An eyewitness stated The car turned over as it crashed into the tree, just missing three people ...

47 The following classes are out on a school trip today Class 6L, Class 6T and Class 6M.

48 The local paper reported School flooded, children sent home.

The following words end in either *ent* or *ant*. Add the correct ending to each word.

49 eleg_____    50 prud_____    51 adjac_____

52 abund_____    53 arrog_____    54 extravag_____

55 contin_____    56 immigr_____    57 cem_____

Circle the **diminutives**.

58–64  golden      gosling      classroom     penknife

statuette   droplet      daylight      hamlet

duckling    starlet      appearance    majorette

Write the possessive form of each of the following.

65 food for the rabbit        _____

66 hairbrush for Leanne       _____

67 football for the players   _____

68  café for the museum  _____

69  handlebar of a bicycle  _____

70  newspaper for Mr Dodd  _____

Improve these **sentences** by changing the group of words in bold for a single one.

71  The children were delighted to be able to talk to the **person who wrote the book**. _____

72  The teacher put the **pens, rulers, pencils and rubbers** in the cupboard.

_____

73  Peter **said he was sorry** for what he had done. _____

74  The weather has improved **during the last day or two**. _____

75  The children who were **at school that day** put up the decorations.

_____

76  Gareth thought it **a waste of time** to copy the words of the song when he could already sing it perfectly.

_____

Add *cious* or *tious* to spell these words correctly.

77  pre_____     78  ficti_____

79  mali_____   80  nutri_____

81  vi_____

Write words with the following number of syllables.

82–83  5 syllables  _____   _____

84–85  6 syllables  _____   _____

Rewrite the passage, adding the missing punctuation. Start new lines where necessary.

**86–100** I will buy you some new shoes said Mum but not until you have out-grown the ones you are wearing now But these aren't fashionable complained Sam Nobody has shoes like these now Mum just laughed

*Now go to the Progress Chart to record your score!* Total 100

# Paper 5

The Adventures of Huckleberry Finn *was written by Mark Twain. His real name was Samuel Clemens but he chose the name 'Mark Twain' while working as a Mississippi river pilot. It was a term used for a water depth of 2 fathoms at which it was considered safe to sail along. After working on the river he then became a reporter, until finally spending his time as an author. He lived from 1835 to 1910.*

*The character Huckleberry Finn was one of an outcast. He was abandoned by his father at a young age. He never wished for a 'normal' life of going to school and having home-comforts around; instead, he liked the freedom to spend his days however he wanted, living close to nature. This produced many an adventure!*

We judged that three more nights would fetch us to Cairo, at the bottom of Illinois, where the Ohio River comes in, and that was what we was after. We would sell the raft and get on a steamboat and go way up the Ohio amongst the free States, and then be out of trouble.

Well, the second night a fog begun to come on, and we made for a tow-head to tie to, for it wouldn't do to try to run in fog; but when I paddled ahead in the canoe, with the line, to make fast, there warn't anything but little saplings to tie to. I passed the line around one of them right on the edge of the cut bank, but there was a stiff current, and the raft come booming down so lively she tore it out by but the roots and away she went. I see the fog closing down, and it made me so sick and scared I couldn't budge for most a half a minute it seemed to me – and then there warn't no raft in sight; you couldn't see twenty yards. I jumped into the canoe and run back to the stem and grabbed the paddle and set her back a stroke. But she didn't come. I was in such a hurry I hadn't untied her. I got up and tried to untie her, but I was so excited my hands shook so I couldn't hardly do anything with them.

As soon as I got started I took out after the raft, hot and heavy, right down the tow-head. That was all right as far as it went, but the tow-head warn't sixty yards long, and the minute I flew by the foot of it I shot out into the solid white fog, and hadn't no more idea which way I was going than a dead man.

Thinks I, it won't do to paddle; first I know I'll run into the bank or a tow-head or something; I got to set still and float, and yet it's mighty fidgety business to have to hold your hands still at such a time. I whooped and listened. Away down there, somewheres, I hear a small whoop, and up comes my spirits. I went tearing after it, listening sharp to hear it again. The next time it come, I see I warn't heading for it but heading away to the right of it. And the next time, I was heading away to the left of it – and not gaining on it much, either, for I was flying around, this way and that and t'other, but it was going straight ahead all the time.

I did wish the fool would think to beat a tin pan, and beat it all the time, but he never did, and it was the still places between the whoops that was making the trouble for me. Well, I fought along, and directly I hears the whoop *behind* me. I was tangled good, now. That was somebody else's whoop, or else I was turned around.

I throwed the paddle down. I heard the whoop again; it was behind me yet, but in a different place; it kept coming, and kept changing its place, and I kept answering, till by-and-by it was in front of me again and I knowed the current had swung the canoe's head down-stream and I was all right, if that was Jim and not some other raftsman hollering. I couldn't tell nothing about voices in a fog, for nothing don't look natural nor sound natural in a fog.

From *The Adventures of Huckleberry Finn* by Mark Twain

Answer these questions.

1 Where did Mark Twain get the idea for his name?

_____

2 Huckleberry Finn was an 'outcast'. Describe what is meant by 'outcast'.

_____

3 Where was Huckleberry Finn heading? _____

4 With whom was Huckleberry Finn travelling? _____

5 On which night did the fog descend? _____

6 The river current is described as 'stiff' (line 8). Which event in the passage illustrates this?

_____

7–8 Find two pieces of evidence from the passage that help us appreciate how thick the fog was.

_____

_____

9–10 Huckleberry Finn felt 'scared' and 'excited' in this passage. Describe why you think he felt each of these emotions.

scared_____

excited_____

11 Why was Huckleberry Finn travelling at night?

_____

12 Find a word in the passage that means 'shouting' or 'shouted'. _____

13 What was Huckleberrry Finn frightened would happen as he untied the canoe and began to move?

_____

14–16 Which three things combined made Huckleberry Finn feel so lost in the canoe while trying to track the sound?

_____

_____

_____

17 Why do you think 'nothing don't look natural nor sound natural in a fog' (lines 36–37)?

_____

**18–20** In your own words describe Huckleberry Finn's character. Use two pieces of evidence from the passage to support your answer.

_____

_____

_____

To each **verb** add an **adverb** that could describe it.

21 spent _____    22 ate _____

23 shone _____    24 remembered _____

25 listened _____    26 wrote _____

27 fought _____    28 helped _____

Complete each **sentence** with the correct **homophone**.

**29–30 enquiry    inquiry**

The politician wanted an _____ into the way an _____ was made about his private life.

**31–32 formally    formerly**

The headteacher _____ requested Mrs. Frampton, _____ a pupil of the school, to join the school governors.

**33–34 beach    beech**

The _____ tree was in a garden quite near the _____.

Match these words with their meanings. Write the number of the correct **definition** by each word.

    (1) a single rail track
    (2) a series of sounds of the same pitch
    (3) a single colour: black and white
    (4) a word of one syllable
    (5) design using initials of a name
    (6) a speech performed by one actor
    (7) one large block of stone

35 monochrome _____    36 monogram _____

37 monolith _____    38 monologue _____

39 monorail _____   40 monosyllable _____

41 monotone _____

Add a **prefix** to make each of these words into its **antonym**.

42 lock _____   43 polite _____

44 agree _____   45 capable _____

46 regular _____   47 own _____

48 reliable _____

Rewrite these sentences changing them from **plural** to **singular**.

49–51 The mice lived in the old barn until the children found them.

_____

52–54 The classes lined up quietly once their teachers had arrived.

_____

55–59 The satsumas were eaten quickly by the children, who then wanted some chocolates!

_____

_____

60–65 Put these words in reverse **alphabetical order**.

transfuse   transference   transfusion   transfer   transfigure   transformer

60 (1) _____   61 (2) _____   62 (3) _____

63 (4) _____   64 (5) _____   65 (6) _____

Rewrite the sentence and punctuate the passage correctly.

66–75 What time are you going home? said Jill to her brother I don't want to be late Tim replied Ill go when you are ready

_____

_____

_____

Answers will vary for questions that require children to answer in their own words. Possible answers to most of these questions are given in *italics*.

## Paper 1

1. The moon had shown itself.
2. Laurie's brother
3–5. *"our scarves were pearled with our breath"; "Hanging branches of willow, manacled in the ice"; "The dead sticks on the ground were easily seen, glittering with the night's new frost"; "We thought of caves, warm skins and fires"*
6–7. *When hands are very cold they take a while to feel warm again. Laurie knew they would get warm but was tormented by the pain until they did.*
8–9. *Laurie's mother is concerned, caring, sympathetic and loving, as illustrated in this line from the passage: "Then there were 'Where've-you-beens?', 'Never-minds', 'Oh-Dears', and 'Come-by-the-fire-you-look-half-dead'."*
10. Stroud
11–12. *because their voices were high-pitched, and they were speaking quickly about the dramatic events they had seen*
13. *Laurie's description of the heavy snowfall illustrates his love for it. "There were millions of tons of the lovely stuff, plastic, pure, all-purpose, which nobody owned, which one could carve or tunnel, eat, or just throw about."*
14. gift, perk
15. They are related to seasonal activities when money is given.
16. bounty
17. *They are the looks of people who have already given some money away and so don't have much left to give.*
18. *a reaction you don't have to think about, an impulse*
19–20. "Coming carol-barking then?" and "For a year we had praised the Lord out of key"
21. provisions
22. entrance
23. choice
24. advertisement
25. performance
26. bewilderment
27. destruction
28. applause
29. decorator
30. cellar
31. plumber
32. disaster
33. corridor
34. burglar
35. popular
36. circular
37. divisor
38. director
39. proprietor
40. partner
41–45. Dad said that **he was** going to mow the lawn. **He hoped** this **would be** the last time **he would** have to do it this year as **he was** tired of doing it.
46–47. They're, their
48–49. their, They're
50–51. There, there
52–53. There, their
54. they've
55. I'd
56. won't
57. adjective
58. verb
59. noun
60. adverb
61–63. *lighthouse, firelight, sunlight*
64–66. *snowdrop, snowfall, snowball*
67–69. *daylight, daydream, daytime*
70. post<u>a</u>ge
71. sent<u>e</u>nce
72. parli<u>a</u>ment
73. m<u>a</u>chinery
74. fatt<u>e</u>ning
75. math<u>e</u>matics
76. hist<u>o</u>ry
77–80. The men were cleaning their houses.
81–82. They jumped over the puddles.
83–86. They bought scarves to support their football teams.
87. principal
88. passed
89. rode
90. whose
91. waste
92. route
93. prey
94. to
95. course
96–100. Sam was caught, thank goodness, otherwise I would have been blamed for stealing the sweets, pen, magazine, Harry Potter book and racing car.

## Paper 2

1. seventy miles per hour
2. left wing
3. two thousand feet
4. *amazing, determined, huge*
5. *the difference between having and then losing control of his situation*
6. because travelling at the speed Jonathan was, to crash into the sea was like hitting a wall of bricks
7–8. "the weight of failure was even heavier on his back" and "drag him gently down to the bottom, and end it all."
9. *from now on*
10. falcon
11. "I am limited by my nature" or "as a poor limited seagull"
12–13. *Jonathan was not alert to listen to the hollow voice because he was so tied up in his own thoughts, taking in the new experience. This is shown in*

the line "The moon and the lights twinkling on the water …".
- 14 because their sight isn't equipped for night flying; their brains aren't made to make night flying easy or safe
- 15 because he realised that the solution to his problem was that he needed short wings like a falcon; because he had just solved his problem
- 16–17 because Jonathan looked grey under the moonlight and he was travelling at a tremendous speed like a cannonball
- 18–20 a description that might include the following words or ideas: *focused, determined, perfectionist, content, assured, confident, different, striving, wants to be better than others, wants to stretch himself as much as possible, wants to be the first to do something different/difficult, stubborn, arrogant*
- 21 mice
- 22 stories
- 23 cargoes or cargos
- 24 thieves
- 25 trolleys
- 26 potatoes
- 27 gases
- 28 oxen
- 29 roofs
- 30 valleys
- 31 6
- 32 4
- 33 3
- 34 1
- 35 5
- 36 2
- 37–46 cook, crutch, lanyard, wedge, movement, ashore, heaviest, deck, spaces, walk
- 47 two peas
- 48 bat
- 49 cucumber
- 50 pie
- 51 gold
- 52 lead
- 53 cricket
- 54 hatter
- 55 Ian <u>had</u> a large appetite.
- 56 Rachel <u>wrote</u> the invitations to her party neatly.
- 57 She intently <u>watched</u> the TV programme.
- 58 Softly she <u>sang</u> the lilting tune.
- 59 They <u>got up</u> early on Sunday.
- 60–61 He <u>lifted</u> the kitten carefully and <u>put</u> it in the basket.
- 62 expand
- 63 export
- 64 decrease
- 65 coarse, thick
- 66 free
- 67 permanent
- 68–71 4 sentences, each with a modal verb e.g. might, will, can, must, should
- 72 crept
- 73 lost
- 74 spoke
- 75 rang
- 76 broke
- 77–83 **They** jumped into the car before **it** sped off at high speed. Joseph whispered that **his** mum had never been so cross. **She** reminded **him** of a bull! **They** agreed with **him**.
- 84–88 "What about the horse? You don't mention sending that back," said Thorin.
- 89–91 *[3 words, each with the prefix 'dis' – e.g. disloyal, discontinue, displease]*
- 92–94 *[3 words, each with the prefix 'mis' – e.g. misunderstand, mislead, misplace]*
- 95 adjective
- 96 noun
- 97 verb
- 98 adverb
- 99 verb
- 100 adjective

## Paper 3

- 1 a snake
- 2 straight
- 3 *in the way the snake looked at/acknowledged the onlooker*
- 4 *during the day*
- 5–7 mused – *pondered*
venomous – *poisonous*
perversity – *strangeness; opposite of what is expected/acceptable*
- 8 'On the day of Sicilian July, with Etna smoking' or 'For in Sicily the black, black snakes are innocent, the gold are venomous.'
- 9 soft-bellied; two-forked tongue; flickered his tongue like a forked night
- 10 The onlooker felt honoured because the snake had chosen his water trough to drink from.
- 11 The earth is described as 'secret' as it is unknown to the onlooker. It is the snake's domain.
- 12–13 The onlooker feels scared, is confused about his/her feelings about the snake, although has great respect for it. "And yet those voices: If you were not afraid, you would kill him!"; "And truly I was afraid, I was most afraid, But even so, honoured still more".
- 14–15 The snake is relaxed, unhurried: "He drank enough and lifted his head, dreamily, as one who has drunken"; "And slowly turned his head"; "And slowly, very slowly, as if thrice adream, proceeded to draw his slow length curving round".
- 16 The log is described as 'clumsy' because logs aren't easy objects to throw with precision and speed.
- 17 The onlooker threw the log as she/he felt braver with the snake's back turned; for a brief second the onlooker wanted to show the snake that she/he was mightier than it; the onlooker gave in to what she/he had been taught about snakes being seen as dangerous and needing to be killed.
- 18–19 hot, dry, "On a hot, hot day, and I in pyjamas for the heat"; "from the burning bowels of the earth"
- 20 The main point is that one shouldn't always give way to what one has been told, but question actions before participating in them.

| | | |
|---|---|---|
| 21–27 | athlete, student, friend, typist, knitter, child, cat | |
| 28 | north east | |
| 29 | public limited company | |
| 30 | please turn over | |
| 31 | department | |
| 32 | milligram(s) | |
| 33 | British Summer Time or British Standard Time | |
| 34 | United Kingdom | |
| 35 | for | |
| 36 | in | |
| 37 | on | |
| 38 | on | |
| 39 | for | |
| 40 | at | |
| 41 | by | |
| 42 | up | |
| 43 | foreign | |
| 44 | believe | |
| 45 | achieve | |
| 46 | conceited | |
| 47 | neighbour | |
| 48 | audience | |
| 49 | height | |
| 50 | ceiling | |
| 51 | badly | |
| 52 | slither | |
| 53 | quantity | |
| 54 | woollen | |
| 55 | where | |
| 56 | ugly | |
| 57 | but | |
| 58–59 | helpful, helping | |
| 60–61 | return, returned | |
| 62–63 | collection, collectable | |
| 64 | request | |
| 65 | enter | |
| 66 | discover | |
| 67 | displeasure | |
| 68–76 | Egyptian, David, February, Wales, Denmark, June, Manchester, Tuesday, Britney [note: queen is an incorrect answer as its capitalisation is dependent on context] | |
| 77 | February | |
| 78 | tomorrow | |
| 79 | possess | |
| 80 | government | |
| 81 | punishment | |
| 82 | fragrance | |
| 83 | arrival | |
| 84 | length | |
| 85 | conclusion | |
| 86 | assistance | |
| 87 | Gina didn't swim in the sea. | |
| 88 | There weren't any stars out tonight or There were no stars out tonight. | |
| 89 | The dogs didn't wait. | |
| 90 | The playground wasn't open. | |
| 91 | Caroline didn't want to/a ride in the car. | |
| 92 | Raj's family hadn't won any money on the lottery or Raj's family had won no money on the lottery. | |
| 93–100 | [8 answers from] you're, you've, won't, they'll, they've, haven't, they're, you'll, aren't | |

## Paper 4

| | |
|---|---|
| 1 | pick and freeze vegetables and fruits |
| 2 | *wants to but hasn't yet started; deciding whether to do something or not* |
| 3–5 | *bad for the environment to use the car to get to the shops; the methods used to grow the vegetables can't be controlled; the price you have to pay is fixed by the supermarkets; the freshness is decided by how supermarkets stack/shelve the produce* |
| 6 | carrot |
| 7 | those who already grow their own vegetables |
| 8 | easy |
| 9–11 | *earth for nutrients, seeds to grow, sunshine, water – to provide the right conditions for the seed to become a plant* |
| 12 | *a laid back, relaxed, non-interfering way of growing* |
| 13 | *settling for the best in the surroundings available* |
| 14 | because they need cutting down to provide light for the vegetable patch |
| 15–17 | "When you buy your vegetables, you are a slave"; his description of the grown carrot, "They are sleek, pointed, orange miracles …"; his conviction that "As I said earlier, growing vegetables is easy." |
| 18–20 | *planning where the vegetables will grow, choosing a suitable range of vegetables, preparing the soil for planting, buying seeds, buying garden equipment* |
| 21–23 | *purr, chug, throb* |
| 24–26 | *howl, whoosh, whistle* |
| 27–30 | *[4 answers from] thorough, bough, thought, rough, enough, cough* |
| 31 | *experimental, experimented* |
| 32 | *preferring, preferred* |
| 33 | *excitable, excitement* |
| 34 | *thoughtless, thoughtful* |
| 35 | *deferred, deferring* |
| 36 | *marriage, married* |
| 37 | *excellence, excellent* |
| 38 | *boredom, bored* |
| 39 | *See you later.* |
| 40 | *You're making fun of me!* |
| 41 | *Did you take the day off school?* |
| 42 | *It was a very good concert.* |
| 43 | *You look good in those sunglasses.* |
| 44 | The following children are absent today: Amina, Ilesh, Frank, Michael and Fayza. |
| 45 | The school magazine reported: No school uniform for a day! |
| 46 | An eyewitness stated: The car turned over as it crashed into the tree, just missing three people … |
| 47 | The following classes are out on a school trip today: Class 6L, Class 6T and Class 6M. |
| 48 | The local paper reported: School flooded, children sent home. |
| 49 | elegant |
| 50 | prudent |
| 51 | adjacent |
| 52 | abundant |
| 53 | arrogant |
| 54 | extravagant |
| 55 | continent |

## ANSWERS

56 immigrant
57 cement
58–64 gosling, statuette, droplet, hamlet, duckling, starlet, majorette
65 the rabbit's food
66 Leanne's hairbrush
67 the players' football
68 the museum's café
69 a bicycle's handlebar
70 Mr Dodd's newspaper
71 author or writer
72 stationery
73 apologised
74 recently or lately
75 present
76 unnecessary or pointless or futile
77 precious
78 fictitious
79 malicious
80 nutritious
81 vicious
82–85 *[words with the correct number of syllables]*
86–100 "I will buy you some new shoes," said Mum, "but not until you have out–grown the ones you are wearing now."
"But these aren't fashionable," complained Sam. "Nobody has shoes like these now."
Mum just laughed.

## Paper 5

1 while working as a Mississippi river pilot; from the term used to mean two fathoms; from the term used to mean that the water was deep enough for it to be safe to sail along
2 *A person who has been driven out of a group or rejected by society.*
3 Cairo
4 Jim
5 the second
6 when Huckleberry Finn ties the boat to some saplings but the current pulls the saplings out
7–8 "you couldn't see twenty yards" and "solid white fog"
9–10 scared – *because in the hostile conditions he had to find Jim*
excited – *because of the difficult conditions and the speed he had to work at in order to track down Jim*
11 because he was in some kind of trouble and at night he couldn't be spotted so easily
12 'hollering' or 'whooped'
13 He was frightened that he would run into something.
14–16 the darkness, the fog and the strength of the current
17 *When in fog your senses are confused as you can't see as well, so things can look and sound strange.*
18–20 an account of Huckleberry Finn's character using evidence from the passage to support the answer; *vulnerable "it made me so sick and scared", resourceful "We would sell the raft", relatively calm, determined*
21 *recklessly*
22 *greedily*
23 *brilliantly*
24 *vaguely*
25 *attentively*
26 *neatly*
27 *bravely*
28 *carefully*
29–30 inquiry; enquiry
31–32 formally; formerly
33–34 beech, beach
35 3
36 5
37 7
38 6
39 1
40 4
41 2
42 unlock
43 impolite
44 disagree
45 incapable
46 irregular
47 disown
48 unreliable
49–51 The mouse lived in the old barn until the child found it.
52–54 The class lined up quietly once its teacher had arrived.
55–59 The satsuma was eaten quickly by the child, who then wanted a chocolate!
60 transfusion
61 transfuse
62 transformer
63 transfigure
64 transference
65 transfer
66–75 "What time are you going home?" said Jill to her brother. "I don't want to be late."
Tim replied, "I'll go when you are ready."
76–87 [*a clause, a section of a sentence with a verb (one mark) using a different connective each time (one mark)*]
88 salmon
89 wife
90 opportunity
91 matrix
92 cactus
93 solo
94 appendix
95 puppy
96–100 [*Each of the hyphenated words correctly written into a sentence*]

## Paper 6

1 at night
2 the road
3 deep red, claret
4 2
5 *It describes the stars twinkling in the sky like jewels.*
6–8 *amount of wealth, intelligence, cleanliness, confidence, speaking ability*

## ANSWERS

9 *because dogs can't speak and in that situation Tim couldn't either*
10–11 The Highwayman was after people's money: "But I shall be back with the yellow gold before the morning light."
12 protectors of the law/law enforcement
13–15 *caring about her appearance, beautiful, black-haired, in love, enjoying excitement/risk, interested in the well-dressed Highwayman, prepared to wait*
16 one that tells a story
17–20 *the way The Highwayman approaches the inn-door; the description of what he looks like; the way he whistled a tune at the landlord's daughter's window; the way he talks to the landlord's daughter and gallops off*
21 ran
22 cassette
23 large
24 cried
25 quickly
26 she
27 loveable or lovable
28 reliable
29 terrible
30 sensible
31 valuable
32 laughable
33 horrible
34 noticeable
35 workable

36–45

| Synonyms | Antonyms |
|---|---|
| vacant/empty | absence/presence |
| tranquil/peaceful | here/there |
| option/choice | coarse/fine |
| famous/noted | seldom/often |
| caution/care | few/many |

46–52 visitor, worker, editor, relation, adult, pupil, passenger
53–54 One morning, as the sun was rising, Jack crept out of the house.
55 In his hand was a small bag, just large enough to carry an apple, two sandwiches and a big slice of cake.
56–57 He turned, looked towards the house, then ran across the field.
58 Jack moved slowly, worried he might be seen.
59–61 As he entered the cave, his eyes adjusting to the darkness, he recognised the silhouette of Aimee, his young and vulnerable sister.
62 communicate
63 secretary
64 conscience
65 environment
66 exaggerate
67 persuasion
68 stomach
69 necessary
70 parliament
71 temperature
72 five tigers' tails
73 nine cows' calves
74 three men's suits
75 four gates' hinges
76 one dog's bone
77 cm
78 kg
79 l
80 mm
81 sq.
82 e.g.
83 no.
84 i.e.
85 I was pleased when the film, <u>frightening and full of suspense</u>, was over!
86 The morning snow, <u>beautiful but cold</u>, had settled outside my bedroom window.
87 The wild horse, <u>dappled grey with a tangled mane</u>, drank silently at the water's edge.
88 Last night's homework, <u>confusing and difficult</u>, took Nina many hours to complete.
89 Our local swimming pool, <u>green, murky and a little smelly</u>, hadn't been cleaned recently.
90 Ben, <u>strong and athletic</u>, was a capable athlete.
91 1
92 3
93 2
94 2
95 3
96 1
97 Capital punishment no longer takes place in Great Britain; it is still used in America.
98 Helen loves doing homework; Laura prefers to socialise.
99 We visited the crown jewels; jewels indeed fit for a queen.
100 An art gallery in London has a collection of Monet pictures; an exhibition which is simply too good to miss.

## Paper 7

1 Buckinghamshire
2 Dahl's wife/widow
3–4 the chocolate doors and foil ball of chocolate wrappers
5 *because it is a very modern museum that uses the latest technology and celebrates children getting involved*
6 Boy
7 *because it might remind them of their school days*
8 in the 1970s
9 *Dahl is saying to those that cast aside the possibilities of magic that unless they open their minds to it they will never know if it is possible or not.*
10–11 *A visit to the toilet at this museum is accompanied with loud sounds and Dahl's voice saying "I will not eat worms!"*
12 *The reporter describes Dahl as 'the great man' as he is known to be one of the greatest children's authors of his generation.*
13 large buildings
14–16 Roald Dahl would approve of this museum because it appeals to children's imaginations, it is state-of-

# ANSWERS

the-art, and it is interactive. Evidence from the article: *"it's the BFG's dream bottle in the centre of the room that has children flocking"; "Everything is designed to be opened and closed, twiddled and fiddled"; "you acted out the stories too, and that was really funny."*

17–18 [child's own description of the type of person Dahl was, e.g. *fun, strange, imaginative, hardworking, wise etc.* Evidence taken from the article to support their answer]

19–20 parents/people who want to know about places they can take children, because the article explains what types of activity are there for children

21 rain
22 tried
23 slept
24 felt
25 saw
26 found
27 met
28 built
29 began
30 The teachers' cars
31 My cousin's cat
32 The children's umbrellas
33 The woman's bank account
34 The singers' guitars
35 The dentist's chair
36 The flats' walls
37 confidential
38 initial
39 essential
40 artificial
41 financial
42 commercial
43 *over*
44 *with*
45 *from*
46 *along*
47 *under*
48 *above*
49 *by*
50 *for*
51 signify
52 happy
53 duty
54 prestige
55 heavy
56 date
57 depend
58 confess

59–69 Saturday, Obedience, remain, owners, several, toy, terriers, hounds, judges, animals, prizes

70 is
71 have
72 is
73 are
74 is
75 are
76 Welsh
77 Tibetan
78 Dutch
79 Portuguese

80–92 Jacob was beginning to get worried; he hadn't heard them for at least five minutes. Jacob called "Is that you, Sandy? Please answer if it is."
"Of course it is! Who else would it be?" responded Sandy, giggling.
(or "Of course it is. ...)

93–100 [completion of the table with words with the correct number of syllables]

## Paper 8

1 Land of Everlasting Winter
2 a giant eagle
3 Gudrun
4 a piece of dark
5 Cark!
6 No Man's Land
7 *The kingdom no longer has any dark, hence there is no night to ride through.*
8–9 *Gudrun felt comforted (she saw familiar faces), tired (she began to become sleepy) and entranced (she forgot what she had come for).*
10 *Houniman meant that whether they could get dark from No Man's Land or not it was too dangerous to stay there. They would have to look elsewhere.*
11 *The story was titled 'The Cost of Night' because the people of King Merrion's kingdom realised how important night was to them.*
12–15 Lord of Winter – *giant eagle, grumpy, angry, cold*
old woman – *hungry, grumpy, bad-tempered*
uncle poet – *focused on task, absent-minded*
All three seem unhappy, not content.
16–20 animals in the story speak and act as humans; concept of dark as something that can be taken by someone; magical/unreal events presented as if common happenings; the poet is able to draw out mist like long threads; land where words freeze
21 adhere
22 accelerate
23 abandon or abscond
24 acute
25 alter or alteration
26 abundant
27 abbreviate or abridge
28 attempt

29–40

| Nouns | Verbs | Adjectives |
|---|---|---|
| reality | expect | carefree |
| uncertainty | caught | happy |
| energy | drown | foolish |
| sunlight | met | artificial |

41 impatient
42 illegible
43 irresponsible
44 discontented
45 uninformed, misinformed
46 nonsense
47 inconsiderate
48 uncertain

49–55 As the water trickled off the roof, on to the path and down into the ever increasing stream, Mark wished it would stop raining. Usually a patient boy, he wouldn't have minded being trapped in the club house if he wasn't supposed to have been home ages ago. Mark had left with Tony, Matt, Anil and Rick but had to return as he had forgotten, in all the excitement, his football kit.
56 dynasties
57 surveys
58 frequencies
59 injuries
60 galleries
61 melodies
62 anthologies
63 photocopies
64–66 The young cat, full of fun, killed the mouse; Dad was pleased.
67 The aircraft was nearly empty; empty seats are good for passengers but bad news for airlines.
68 Polar bears are beginning to move closer to people's homes; it can't be long before there is an attack.
69–71 Rugby training is hard work; we start with a run, continue with 30 press-ups, practise moves and finish with a training match.
72 active
73 active
74 passive
75 active
76 passive
77–82 [answers each describing the metaphors]
83 sil**e**ntly
84 pris**o**n
85 dicti**o**nary
86 nurs**e**ry
87 comp**a**ny
88 choc**o**late
89 diff**e**rent
90 fragr**a**nce
91 temp**e**rature
92–94 [each sentence completed as a conditional sentence. A conditional sentence is a sentence that expresses the idea that one thing depends on something else e.g. *Sundeep will go to the shop or he won't have any bread for lunch tomorrow.*]
95 better
96 latest
97 worse
98 least
99–100 harder, cleverer

## Paper 9

1 "occasions of great public rejoicing"
2 three months
3 basin/porringer
4 to catch any stray splashes of gruel
5 *They held a meeting.*
6–7 *One boy suggested he might eat the boy that slept next to him, he was so hungry. Oliver was chosen at random, 'lots were cast'.*
8 *He was so miserable and hungry that he would risk anything for some more food.*
9 *extreme boldness*
10 *It emphasises the difference between him and the thin, ill, starving boys.*
11–13 *Mr Bumble's violence is illustrated when hitting out at Oliver when he asked for more, etc.*
14–15 [child's description of the room in which Oliver was imprisoned: *dark, gloomy, cold, bare, etc.*]
16 hang himself
17–18 [child's reaction to the final sentence of the passage: *the last sentence makes me feel sad and worried for Oliver because he is desperate for someone to love and take care of him. This is shown when he tries to curl up to the wall, wanting someone to protect and help him.*]
19–20 *The punishment seems excessive for the crime of asking for more food. It suggests that those in charge of the boys were actually afraid of them and needed to keep them in such a way that they ruled them by fear; those in charge had little feeling for the boys or for the fact that they were only children.*
21 anxious
22 perilous
23 regional
24 choral
25 methodical
26 long
27 ornamental
28 metallic
29 duck's back
30 china shop
31 fiddle
32 March hare or hatter or coot
33 church mouse
34 dodo or doornail
35 sauce
36 altar
37 source
38 practice
39 stationary
40 practise
41 alter
42 desert
43 stationery
44 dessert
45–50 [a clause (a section of a sentence with a verb) added to each of the sentences, e.g. *My friend knows more about horses than I do, which is a good thing since she lives on a farm.*]
51 has
52 should
53 comes
54 here
55 are
56 will
57 says
58 shall
59 the cat's tail
60 the five children's coats
61 the apple's pips or the apples' pips
62 the three dogs' bones

| | | | | |
|---|---|---|---|---|
| 63 | the seven houses' keys | | 32 | until |
| 64 | the video's case | | 33 | unless |
| 65 | the four horses' foals | | 34 | because |
| 66 | the six computers' keyboards | | 35 | **r**hythm |
| 67 | herd | | 36 | rei**g**n |
| 68 | plague or swarm | | 37 | **k**not |
| 69 | pride | | 38 | **r**hombus |
| 70 | band or group | | 39 | colum**n** |
| 71 | litter | | 40 | **h**our |
| 72 | flock | | 41 | hym**n** |
| 73 | murder | | 42 | **g**uard |

**ANSWERS**

74–81 engagement, alignment, membership, receivership, censorship, scholarship, enhancement, contentment

82–96 It was **S**unday afternoon, the sun was glinting through the trees and it was warm. **A**melia called to **G**eorge, "**A**re we going to do something today**?** **I**'m bored of just sitting here." **H**e ignored her**.**

97–100 [a mnemonic (a way of remembering a particular spelling) for each of the four words listed, e.g. WEIGHT – W plus eight]

## Paper 10

1 Princess Beatrice
2 in her sitting-room at Kensington Palace
3 uncle
4–5 desirous – *wanting, having a desire, desiring* condolence – *sympathy*
6–7 *pleased, proud, determined, excited*
8–9 *She would have expressed her sympathy and her fondness for her uncle. Evidence from the extract: "whom I charged to express my feelings of condolence and sorrow to the poor Queen".*
10 1 year and 8 days.
11–12 the nerves and excitement of the day ahead
13 because the crown was about to be placed on her head
14 *Victoria described herself as loaded as at this point she was wearing and holding all the required articles for the Coronation.*
15 Dalmatic robe
16–17 *In those days television hadn't been invented, so to watch and be part of such an important occasion people had to actually attend; people would want to be a part of an historic event; people wanted to see the new Queen; people wanted to show the new Queen that they supported her.*
18–20 evidence from the extract highlighting how Victoria felt at her Coronation: *"shall ever remember this day as the proudest of my life"*

| | | |
|---|---|---|
| 21–22 | censure | **praise** |
| 23–24 | raise | **lower** |
| 25–26 | gather | **disperse** |
| 27–28 | increase | **contract** |
| 29–30 | minimum | **most** |
| 31 | whether | |

43 active
44 passive
45 active
46 active
47 active
48 passive
49 passive
50 3
51 6
52 5
53 2
54 7
55 8
56 1
57 4
58–65 [words in bold used in both a statement (a formal account of facts) and then a question]
66–67 far off      e.g. *television*
68–69 small or millionth   e.g. *microphone* or *micrometre*
70–71 below or under    e.g. *submerge*
72–73 water     e.g. *aquamarine*
74–75 self      e.g. *autograph*
76 from
77 on
78 to
79 beyond
80 on
81 outside
82 up
83–86 [four sentences, each with a colon (a colon is used to show that what follows is an example quotation, list or summary of what precedes it).]
87 fought
88 built
89 ran
90 got
91 meant
92 became
93 found
94 felt
95 interesting
96 unfortunately
97 specification
98 infrastructure
99 rehearsal
100 independence

Add a **clause** to each of these to make a longer **sentence**. Use a different **connective** each time.

**76–77** Zoe sprinted, just staying ahead _____

**78–79** Zoe sprinted, just staying ahead _____

**80–81** Zoe sprinted, just staying ahead _____

**82–83** Jack kept his eyes firmly on the ground _____

**84–85** Jack kept his eyes firmly on the ground _____

**86–87** Jack kept his eyes firmly on the ground _____

Write these words in their **singular** form.

**88** salmon  _____   **89** wives  _____

**90** opportunities  _____   **91** matrices  _____

**92** cacti  _____   **93** solos  _____

**94** appendices  _____   **95** puppies  _____

Write each of these hyphenated words correctly in a **sentence**.

**96** empty-handed _____

**97** self-assured _____

**98** spine-chilling _____

**99** deep-fried _____

**100** hair-raising _____

*Now go to the Progress Chart to record your score!* Total / 100

# Paper 6

The wind was a torrent of darkness among the gusty trees,
The moon was a ghostly galleon tossed upon cloudy seas,
The road was a ribbon of moonlight over the purple moor,
And the highwayman came riding –
   Riding – riding –                                         5
The highwayman came riding, up to the old inn-door.

He'd a French cocked-hat on his forehead, a bunch of lace at his chin,
A coat of claret velvet, and breeches of brown doe skin;
They fitted with never a wrinkle: his boots were up to the thigh!
And he rode with a jewelled tinkle,                   10
   His pistol butts a-twinkle,
His rapier hilt a-twinkle, under the jewelled sky.

Over the cobbles he clattered and clashed in the dark inn-yard,
And he tapped with his whip on the shutters, but all was locked and barred;
He whistled a tune to the window, and who should be waiting there        15
But the landlord's black-eyed daughter,
   Bess, the landlord's daughter,
Plaiting a dark red love-knot into her long black hair.

And dark in the old inn-yard a stable-wicket creaked
Where Tim the ostler listened; his face was white and peaked;        20
His eyes were hollows of madness, his hair like mouldy hay,
But he loved the landlord's daughter,
   The landlord's red-lipped daughter;
Dumb as a dog he listened, and he heard the robber say –

'One kiss, my bonny sweetheart, I'm after a prize tonight,        25
But I shall be back with the yellow gold before the morning light;
Yet, if they press me sharply, and harry me through the day,
Then look for me by moonlight,
   Watch for me by moonlight,
I'll come to thee by moonlight, though hell should bar the way.'       30

He rose upright in the stirrups; he scarce could reach her hand,
But she loosened her hair i' the casement! His face burnt like a brand
As the black cascade of perfume came tumbling over his breast;
And he kissed its waves in the moonlight,
   (Oh, sweet black waves in the moonlight!)        35
Then he tugged at his rein in the moonlight, and galloped away to the west.

From *The Highwayman* by Alfred Noyes

Answer these questions.

1 At what time of day was this poem set? _____

2 What was 'a ribbon of moonlight'? _____

**3** What colour was The Highwayman's coat? _____

**4** How many people do we know were in love with the landlord's daughter?

_____

**5** Explain what is meant by the words 'jewelled sky' (line 12).

_____

**6–8** Highlight three distinct differences between The Highwayman and Tim.

_____

_____

_____

**9** Why do you think Tim was described as 'Dumb as a dog' (line 24)?

_____

_____

**10–11** What prize do you think The Highwayman was after? Which line in the passage conveys this?

_____

_____

**12** Who might 'harry' (line 27) The Highwayman?

_____

**13–15** How would you describe the landlord's daughter, as shown in the poem?

_____

_____

_____

**16** The Highwayman is a narrative poem. What is a narrative poem?

_____

**17–20** Explore the ways in which the poet creates the sense of confidence surrounding The Highwayman. Support your answer with lines from the poem.

_____

_____

Underline the word which is the same part of speech as the word in bold.

| 21 | **laughed** | loudly | longer | ran | wild | joker |
| 22 | **magazine** | entered | cassette | he | wrote | her |
| 23 | **tiny** | bee | wasp | flew | away | large |
| 24 | **sang** | cried | loudly | nice | silently | nation |
| 25 | **loudly** | quickly | quieten | quicken | game | film |
| 26 | **they** | boys | children | she | teacher | class |

Add the **suffix** *able* or *ible* to the words.

27 love _____   28 rely _____   29 terror _____

30 sense _____   31 value _____   32 laugh _____

33 horror _____   34 notice _____   35 work _____

Some of the following pairs of words are **synonyms** and some are **antonyms**. Put them in the correct columns in the table.

36–45      vacant/empty    absence/presence    tranquil/peaceful

option/choice    seldom/often    few/many    here/there

caution/care    coarse/fine    famous/noted

| Synonyms | Antonyms |
|---|---|
|  |  |
|  |  |
|  |  |
|  |  |
|  |  |

Underline any word below which does not have a specifically feminine form.
    **Example**   actor → actress    builder → no specific feminine form

46–52      visitor    hero    waiter    worker

manager    editor    relation    widower

adult    mayor    pupil    passenger

Add the missing commas to these sentences.

**53–54** One morning as the sun was rising Jack crept out of the house.

**55** In his hand was a small bag just large enough to carry an apple two sandwiches and a big slice of cake.

**56–57** He turned looked towards the house then ran across the field.

**58** Jack moved slowly worried he might be seen.

**59–61** As he entered the cave his eyes adjusting to the darkness he recognised the silhouette of Aimee his young and vulnerable sister.

Spell these words correctly.

**62** comunicate      **63** secretery

**64** consience      **65** enviroment

**66** exagerate      **67** persasion

**68** stomache      **69** necesary

**70** parliment      **71** temperture

Copy and add the missing apostrophes.

**72** five tigers tails

**73** nine cows calves

**74** three mens suits

**75** four gates hinges

**76** one dogs bone

Write the **abbreviation** of each of these.

**77** centimetre      **78** kilogram

**79** litre      **80** millimetre

**81** square      **82** for example

**83** number      **84** that is

Underline the **adjectival phrase** in each **sentence**.

85 I was pleased when the film, frightening and full of suspense, was over!

86 The morning snow, beautiful but cold, had settled outside my bedroom window.

87 The wild horse, dappled grey with a tangled mane, drank silently at the water's edge.

88 Last night's homework, confusing and difficult, took Nina many hours to complete.

89 Our local swimming pool, green, murky and a little smelly, hadn't been cleaned recently.

90 Ben, strong and athletic, was a capable athlete.

These are three ways in which words are derived. Write the appropriate number next to each word to show where you think it came from:

(1) imitating a sound

(2) another language

(3) name of a place or person

91 moo  _____

92 cardigan  _____

93 autograph  _____

94 pizza  _____

95 biro  _____

96 whoosh  _____

Add the missing semicolons to these **sentences**.

97 Capital punishment no longer takes place in Great Britain it is still used in America.

98 Helen loves doing homework Laura prefers to socialise.

99 We visited the crown jewels jewels indeed fit for a queen.

100 An art gallery in London has a collection of Monet pictures an exhibition which is simply too good to miss.

*Now go to the Progress Chart to record your score!* Total / 100

# Paper 7

**A Dahl of a day out**

*For a whizzpopping day out, grab the kids and head for Great Missenden.*

'It even smells like chocolate!' cries Dougie, aged 7, as we enter the Roald Dahl Museum and Story Centre in Great Missenden, Bucks. It looks like I'm onto a winner already. My challenge for the day is to help keep my nephew and his 9-year-old sister Meg entertained during the school holidays. So we've taken a short spin out of London – only 45 minutes or so – up the M40 to find out just how much fun we can have in a museum dedicated to the greatest children's author of his generation.

According to Dahl's widow Liccy, there are four things her late husband really didn't like: beards, committees, speeches and museums. So don't attach too much significance to the word 'Museum' in the title of this place: Roald may not have approved of dusty, fusty edifices with squeaky glossed floors and highly polished glass cabinets, but this hi-tech interactive playground for kids would surely have earned his approval.

As soon as we arrive, children are presented with a booklet entitled 'My Story Ideas'. It has a picture of Dahl scribbling away in his writer's hut on the cover, and as children wend their way round the small but well-designed museum, they are encouraged to use it as a mini-scrapbook, filling it with stamps and pictures as they go round. 'I can finish this when I get home,' says Meg, clutching the book as we charge through the chocolate doors to the first gallery, titled Boy.

This room is the most traditional part of the museum, providing an insight into Dahl's childhood and a peek into his personal archive. There are letters sent home from boarding school, reports ('very much improved' in English composition), and interactive touch-screen computer displays, cleverly designed to look like old school exercise books. These give adults a nostalgia trip while the kids press the screen and get the background info on their hero's work. I could have spent more time here, but the children have other ideas. 'The next room has puppets in it!' says Dougie, who's been checking out what else lies in store.

Inside the Solo gallery, a giant video screen projects images from the movie version of *James and the Giant Peach* to a background of the title music from Dahl's hit TV series from the 1970s, *Tales of the Unexpected*. But, it's the *BFG*'s dream bottle in the centre of the room that has children flocking. Here they create their own puppet shadow display. 'You can make your own show with a crocodile on a stick,' Dougie explains enthusiastically when I ask him what he likes most about this part. Meg meanwhile is investigating the stamps that print Quentin Blake's exquisite illustrations for Dahl's children's books onto card. 'It's a really good idea,' she says, proudly showing me *The Enormous Crocodile* she's just inked onto a postcard that the museum conveniently provides for the kids. The carpet on the floor bears a single line from one of Dahl's notebooks in his barely legible script: 'Those who don't believe in magic will never find it.'

Before heading into the next gallery – the Story Centre of the title – we stop off for a comfort break. 'That gave me a fright', says Dougie, giggling madly as the loo emits an alarming whizzpopping noise, replaced a minute later by the voice of the great man himself declaring, 'I will not eat worms!'

   You can also investigate the inside of a faithful recreation of Dahl's beloved writing hut. Here we discovered some of the precious objects he kept on his desk including a huge ball of foil made up of chocolate bar wrappers that he'd eaten and a piece of his own hip bone removed during an operation ('Yuk!' exclaimed Meg gleefully). Everything is designed to be opened and closed, twiddled and fiddled, so that nosey, interfering children and their equally enquiring parents and guardians can enjoy the play value of the place without being told off – or getting dirty looks from the staff.

   Our last stop is Miss Honey's Schoolroom where it is story time. A couple of energetic young guys acted out tales from Dahl's *Revolting Rhymes* with such infectious enthusiasm that I seriously feared for the health of one young man who puffs so much during *Tale of the Three Little Piggies* that he practically starts hyperventilating. The spellbound audience squeals delightedly as he goes redder and redder in the face. But his performance does not go unappreciated by the young audience. 'I thought you were just going to read to us,' says Dougie afterwards as he chats happily to the reader, 'but you acted out the stories too, and that was really funny.'

Article by Damien Kelleher

Answer these questions.

1 In which county is the museum? _____

2 Who is Liccy? _____

3–4 Find two pieces of evidence in the passage of the museum's links with Dahl's book *Charlie and the Chocolate Factory*.

_____

_____

5 Why is the museum described as a 'hi-tech interactive playground for kids'?

_____

6 In which gallery were Dahl's letters and school reports?

_____

7 Why would interactive displays of old school exercise books give adults a 'nostalgia trip'?

_____

8 When did Roald Dahl have a hit TV series? _____

9  Explain in your own words what Dahl meant by 'Those who don't believe in magic will never find it' (lines 37–38).

_____

10–11  What is a 'comfort break' (line 40) and how is the experience different?

_____
_____

12  Why is Roald Dahl described as 'the great man' (line 42)?

_____

13  What is the meaning of the word 'edifices' on line 10?

_____

14–16  Give three reasons why Roald Dahl would approve of this museum. Use evidence from the article to support your answer.

_____
_____
_____

17–18  Describe the sort of person Roald Dahl is, as shown in this article.

_____
_____

19–20  Who is the intended audience for this article? Explain your answer.

_____
_____

Fill the gap by writing the past tense of the word in bold.

21  **run**  The children _____ as fast as they could in the race.

22  **try**  I wasn't pleased with my score, but I had _____ my best.

23  **sleep**  The noise of the plane meant that I only _____ for a few hours.

24  **feel**  I _____ pleased when I was told that Emma was coming to visit.

25  **see**  When we _____ the presents we were very excited.

26  **find**  Luckily, Jamal _____ his wallet and keys.

**27 meet** We _____ last Wednesday after lunch.

**28 build** The new house on our block was _____ in less than six months.

**29 begin** The concert _____ on time.

Write the possessive form of each of these **phrases**, i.e. with an apostrophe.

    **Example** The funnels of the ships    The ships' funnels

30 The cars of the teachers     _____

31 The cat of my cousin     _____

32 The umbrellas of the children     _____

33 The bank account of the woman     _____

34 The guitars of the singers     _____

35 The chair of the dentist     _____

36 The walls of the flats     _____

Add *cial* or *tial* to spell these words correctly.

37 confiden_____      38 ini_____

39 essen_____      40 artifi_____

41 finan_____      42 commer_____

Complete the following **sentences** by writing a different **preposition** in each space.

43 He climbed _____ the gate with ease.

44 Mark corresponds _____ two penfriends.

45 Granny is suffering _____ arthritis.

46 We walked slowly _____ the river bank.

47 Her paper was hidden _____ the pile of books.

48 Keep your head _____ the water when learning to swim.

49 I put it _____ the radiator.

50 We waited _____ the bus.

Write the root of each of the words.

51 significant _____  52 happiness _____

53 dutiful _____  54 prestigious _____

55 heavily _____  56 predate _____

57 independent _____  58 confession _____

In the following passage there are blanks. The jumbled word in brackets, when the letters are rearranged, makes a word to fill the blank.

59–69 Last _____ (aaurStdy) my friend and I went to a Dog Show.

First we saw the _____ (Obcdeeein) Class. The dogs had to

_____ (narmei) where they were, even though their _____

(swoner) had walked away. There were _____ (verseal) other

classes. One was for _____ (oyt) dogs, another was for

_____ (trrreeis) and a third was for _____ (hsunod). The

_____ (jusdeg) looked carefully at the _____ (slamina) before

awarding the _____ (pzesir).

Underline the correct word in the brackets.
70 Not one of the children (are, is) allowed in the sea.
71 All of you but one (have, has) brothers.
72 Neither of the children (are, is) from this town.
73 All the children (are, is) having a hamburger.
74 Which one of you three (are, is) going to do it?
75 How many of you (are, is) eleven years old?

Fill each blank with an **adjective** based on the name of a country.

76 _____ lamb comes from Wales.

77 _____ rugs are made in Tibet.

78 Holland is the home of the _____ people.

79 _____ people come from Portugal.

41

Copy and punctuate the passage correctly, without affecting lower case or capital letters.

**80–92** Jacob was beginning to get worried he hadn't heard them for at least five minutes Jacob called Is that you Sandy Please answer if it is

Of course it is Who else would it be responded Sandy giggling

Complete the table.

**93–100**

| No. of syllables | Word | | |
|---|---|---|---|
| 3 | | | |
| 4 | | | |
| 5 | dissatisfaction | | |

Now go to the Progress Chart to record your score!

# Paper 8

*A powerful enchanter in the guise of a crocodile, on winning a game of heads or tails against King Merrion the Carefree, requested as his prize all the dark in the King's kingdom. This he was granted but it had a devastating effect. The princess and her greatest friend the horse called Houniman decided to solve the predicament that King Merrion had got them in …*

The princess rode on Houniman and he galloped steadily northwards for seven days and what ought to have been seven nights, over a sea of ice, until they came to the Land of Everlasting Winter, where the words freeze as you speak them, and even thoughts rattle in your head like icicles.

There they found the Lord of Winter, in the form of a giant eagle, brooding on a rock.

'Sir,' called Gudrun from a good way off – for it was so cold in his neighbourhood that the very birds froze in the air and hung motionless – 'can you tell us where we can find a bit of dark?'

He lifted his head with its great hooked beak and gave them an angry look.

'Why should I help you? I have only one little piece of dark, and I am keeping it for myself, under my wing, so that it may grow.'

'Does dark grow?' said Gudrun.

'Of course it grows, stupid girl! Cark! Be off with you!' And the eagle spread one wing (keeping the other tight folded) so that a great white flurry of snow and wind drove towards Gudrun and Houniman, and they turned and galloped away.

At the edge of the Land of Winter they saw an old woman leading a reindeer loaded with wood.

'Mother,' called Gudrun, 'can you tell us where we might find a bit of dark?'

'Give me a piece of bread and cheese for myself and some corn for my beast and I will consider.'

So they gave her the bread and corn and she considered. Presently she said:

'There will be plenty of dark in the past. You should go to No Man's Land, the frontier where the present slips into the past, and perhaps you might be able to pick up a bit of dark there.'

'Good,' said the princess, 'that sounds hopeful. But in which direction does the past lie?'

'Towards the setting sun, of course!' snapped the old woman, and she gave her reindeer a thump to make it jog along faster.

So Gudrun and Houniman turned towards the setting sun and galloped on for seven days and what should have been seven nights, until they reached No Man's Land. This was a strange and misty region, with low hills and marshes; in the middle of it they came to a great lake, on the shore of which sat an old poet in a little garden of cranberry shrubs. Instead of water the lake was filled with blue-grey mist, and the old poet was drawing out the mist in long threads, and twisting them and turning them into poems. It was very silent all around there, with not a living creature, and the old poet was so absorbed in what he did that he never lifted his head until they stood beside him.

'Can you tell us, uncle poet,' said Gudrun, 'where we might pick up a bit of dark?'

'Dark?' he said absently. 'Eh, what's that? You want a bit of dark? There's plenty at the bottom of the lake.'

So Gudrun dismounted and walked to the edge of the lake, and looked down through the mist. Thicker and thicker it grew, darker and darker, down in the depths of the lake, and as she looked down she could see all manner of strange shapes, and some that seemed familiar too – faces that she had once known, places that she had once visited, all sunk down in the dark depths of the past. As she leaned over, the mist seemed to rise up around her, so that she began to become sleepy, to forget who she was and what she had come for…  45

'Gudrun! Come back!' cried Houniman loudly, and he stretched out his long neck and caught hold of her by the hair and pulled her back, just as she was about to topple into the lake.

'Climb on my back and let's get out of here!' he said. 'Dark or no dark, this place is too dangerous!'  50

But Gudrun cried to the poet, 'Uncle poet, isn't there any other place where we might pick up a bit of dark?'

'Dark?' he said. 'You want a bit of dark? Well, I suppose you might try the Gates of Death; dark grows around there.'

*The Cost of Night* by Joan Aiken

Answer these questions.

1 Where do words freeze as you speak?

_____

2 Which animal was the Lord of Winter? _____

3 What is the princess's name? _____

4 What are Houniman and the princess looking for?

_____

5 Find an **onomatopoeic** word used by the Lord of Winter. _____

6 Where does the present slip into the past?

_____

7 Why do Gudrun and Houniman gallop for 'what should have been seven nights' (line 29)?

_____

8–9 Describe in your own words how Gudrun felt at the edge of the lake. Use evidence from the passage to support your answer.

_____

_____

_____

**10** What did Houniman mean when he said, 'Dark or no dark, this place is too dangerous' (lines 49–50)?

_____

**11** The title of this story is 'The Cost of Night'. Why do you think it is called this?

_____

**12–15** The princess and Houniman meet three characters in this passage. Describe briefly each character they meet and make a note of something they all have in common.

_____

_____

_____

_____

**16–20** Describe five events or features of the story that make it a fable.

_____

_____

_____

_____

Write a word, beginning with *a*, which has the same meaning as the word on the left.

| | | | | | |
|---|---|---|---|---|---|
| **21** | stick | ad_____ | **22** | quicken | ac_____ |
| **23** | leave | ab_____ | **24** | sharp | ac_____ |
| **25** | change | al_____ | **26** | plentiful | ab_____ |
| **27** | shorten | ab_____ | **28** | try | at_____ |

Put these words in the correct columns.

**29–40**

| | | | | |
|---|---|---|---|---|
| happy | energy | expect | caught | met |
| uncertainty | drown | foolish | sunlight | reality |
| carefree | artificial | | | |

| Nouns | Verbs | Adjectives |
|---|---|---|
|  |  |  |
|  |  |  |
|  |  |  |
|  |  |  |

Write an **antonym** for each word by adding a **prefix**.

41 patient _____    42 legible _____

43 responsible _____    44 contented _____

45 informed _____    46 sense _____

47 considerate _____    48 certain _____

Add the missing commas to the passage.

49–55 As the water trickled off the roof on to the path and down into the ever increasing stream Mark wished it would stop raining. Usually a patient boy he wouldn't have minded being trapped in the club house if he wasn't supposed to have been home ages ago. Mark had left with Tony Matt Anil and Rick but had to return as he had forgotten in all the excitement his football kit.

Write the **plural** form of each of these words.

56 dynasty _____    57 survey _____

58 frequency _____    59 injury _____

60 gallery _____    61 melody _____

62 anthology _____    63 photocopy _____

Add the missing semicolons and commas to these **sentences**.

64–66 The young cat full of fun killed the mouse Dad was pleased.

67 The aircraft was nearly empty empty seats are good for passengers but bad news for airlines.

68 Polar bears are beginning to move closer to people's homes it can't be long before there is an attack.

69–71 Rugby training is hard work we start with a run continue with 30 press-ups practise moves and finish with a training match.

State whether each of these **sentences** has an **active** or **passive verb**.

72  Brian washed the dishes. _____

73  Janie wrote her diary. _____

74  The cyclist was struck by the lorry. _____

75  Columbus reached America in 1492. _____

76  The moon was first visited by Neil Armstrong. _____

Explain what each of these **metaphors** means.

77  The sky was on fire.

_____

78  The moon was a ghostly galleon.

_____

79  The birds were a joyful choir.

_____

80  The thunder is an angry giant.

_____

81  The clouds were cotton wool.

_____

82  The sea was an angry dog.

_____

Circle the unstressed vowels.

83  silently          84  prison           85  dictionary

86  nursery           87  company          88  chocolate

89  different         90  fragrance        91  temperature

Complete each of these **conditional sentences**.

92  Sundeep will go to the shop _____

93  The battery in your mobile phone will run out _____

94 We might go to the cinema _____

_____

Underline the correct word in brackets.

95 Has Keith or Kim the (good, better, best) bat?

96 Of all the children he was the (late, later, latest) to arrive.

97 The more sweets you eat the (bad, worse, worst) your teeth will be.

98 The (little, less, least) you can expect is to receive a letter.

99–100 The (hard, harder, hardest) you work the (clever, cleverer, cleverest) you will be.

*Now go to the Progress Chart to record your score!* **Total** 100

# Paper 9

The room in which the boys were fed, was a large stone hall, with a copper at one end: out of which the master, dressed in an apron for the purpose, and assisted by one or two women, ladled the gruel at meal-times. Of this festive composition each boy had one porringer, and no more – except on occasions of great public rejoicing, when he had two ounces and a quarter of bread besides. The bowls never wanted washing. The boys polished them with their spoons till they shone again; and when they had performed this operation (which never took very long, the spoons being nearly as large as the bowls), they would sit staring at the copper, with such eager eyes, as if they could have devoured the very bricks of which it was composed; employing themselves, meanwhile, in sucking their fingers most assiduously, with the view of catching up any stray splashes of gruel that might have been cast thereon. Boys have generally excellent appetites. Oliver Twist and his companions suffered the tortures of slow starvation for three months: at last they got so voracious and wild with hunger, that one boy, who was tall for his age, and hadn't been used to that sort of thing (for his father had kept a small cookshop), hinted darkly to his companions, that unless he had another basin of gruel *per diem,* he was afraid he might some night happen to eat the boy who slept next to him, who happened to be a weakly youth of tender age. He had a wild, hungry eye; and they implicitly believed him. A council was held; lots were cast who should walk up to the master after supper that evening, and ask for more; and it fell to Oliver Twist.

The evening arrived; the boys took their places. The master, in his cook's uniform, stationed himself at the copper; his pauper assistants ranged themselves behind him; the gruel was served out; and a long grace was said over the short commons. The gruel disappeared; the boys whispered to each other, and winked at Oliver; while his next neighbours nudged him. Child as he was, he was desperate with hunger, and reckless with misery. He rose from the table; and advancing to the master, basin and spoon in hand, said, somewhat alarmed at his own temerity:

'Please, sir, I want some more.'

The master was a fat, healthy man; but he turned very pale. He gazed in stupefied astonishment on the small rebel for some seconds, and then clung for support to the copper. The assistants were paralysed with wonder; the boys with fear.

'What!' said the master at length, in a faint voice.

'Please, sir,' replied Oliver, 'I want some more.'

The master aimed a blow at Oliver's head with the ladle, pinioned him in his arms, and shrieked aloud for the beadle.

The board were sitting in solemn conclave, when Mr Bumble rushed into the room in great excitement, and addressing the gentleman in the high chair, said,

'Mr Limbkins, I beg your pardon, sir! Oliver Twist has asked for more!' There was a general start. Horror was depicted on every countenance.

'For *more*!' said Mr Limbkins. 'Compose yourself, Bumble, and answer me distinctly. Do I understand that he asked for more, after he had eaten the supper allotted by the dietary?'

'He did, sir,' replied Bumble.

'That boy will be hung,' said the gentleman in the white waistcoat; 'I know that boy will be hung.'

Nobody controverted the prophetic gentleman's opinion. An animated discussion took place. Oliver was ordered into instant confinement; and a bill was next morning pasted on the outside of the gate, offering a reward of five pounds to anybody who would take Oliver Twist off the hands of the parish. In other words, five pounds and Oliver Twist were offered to any man or woman who wanted an apprentice to any trade, business, or calling.

'I never was more convinced of anything in my life,' said the gentleman in the white waistcoat, as he knocked at the gate and read the bill next morning: 'I never was more convinced of anything in my life, than I am that that boy will come to be hung.'…

For a week after the commission of the impious and profane offence of asking for more, Oliver remained a close prisoner in the dark and solitary room to which he had been consigned by the wisdom and mercy of the board. It appears, at first sight, not unreasonable to suppose, that, if he had entertained a becoming feeling of respect for the prediction of the gentleman in the white waistcoat, he would have established that sage individual's prophetic character, once and forever, by tying one end of his pocket-handkerchief to a hook in the wall, and attaching himself to the other. To the performance of this feat, however, there was one obstacle: namely, that pocket-handkerchiefs being decided articles of luxury, had been, for all future times and ages, removed from the noses of paupers by the express order of the board, in council assembled; solemnly given and pronounced under their hands and seals. There was still greater obstacle in Oliver's youth and childishness. He only cried bitterly all day; and, when the long, dismal night came on, spread his little hands before his eyes to shut out the darkness, and crouching in the corner, tried to sleep: ever and anon waking with a start and a tremble, and drawing himself closer and closer to the wall, as if to feel even its cold hard surface were a protection in the gloom and loneliness which surrounded him.

From *Oliver Twist* by Charles Dickens

Answer these questions.

1 When were the boys given bread?

2 For how long had the boys been starving?

3 Find another word in the passage for 'a bowl'. _____

4 Why did the boys suck their fingers?

5 What is meant by 'A council was held' (line 19)?

6–7 Why was it decided someone should ask for more food? How was Oliver chosen?

8 Oliver is described as 'reckless with misery' (line 26). What does this mean?

9 Write a definition for the word 'temerity' (line 27).

50

10  What does the description 'The master was a fat, healthy man' (line 29) emphasise in the context of the dining hall?

_____

_____

11–13  Describe Mr Bumble. Use evidence from the passage to support your answer.

_____

_____

_____

14–15  In your own words, describe the room in which Oliver was imprisoned.

_____

_____

16  What is suggested that Oliver could do with a pocket-handkerchief?

_____

17–18  How does the last sentence of the passage make you feel? Use evidence from the passage to support your answer.

_____

_____

19–20  Do you think Oliver's punishment was appropriate for the crime he committed? What does this tell you about those who carried out the punishment?

_____

_____

From each of the words in bold make an **adjective** to fit the **sentence**.

21  **anxiety**   The _____ woman waited for his return.

22  **peril**     The mountaineers set out on their _____ climb.

23  **region**    They heard the report on the _____ news.

24  **choir**     The _____ society performed at the concert.

25  **method**    They tackled the task in a very _____ way.

26  **length**    Her _____ dress was much admired.

27 **ornament**   The _____ gate was painted white.

28 **metal**   It made a _____ noise when it fell to the ground.

Complete these **similes**.

29 Like water off a _____.

30 Like a bull in a _____.

31 As fit as a _____.

32 As mad as a _____.

33 As poor as a _____.

34 As dead as a _____.

Use the words in bold to fill the gaps.

| sauce | practice | desert | alter | stationary |
| source | practise | dessert | altar | stationery |

35 We all like apple _____ with pork.

36 There were beautiful lilies on the _____.

37 The _____ of the River Dee is in North Wales.

38 I must do some _____.

39 The train was _____; they need not have hurried.

40 The team must _____ their bowling.

41 Miss Bell must _____ her timetable.

42 The Sahara _____ is in Africa.

43 "You will need more _____ to write all those letters."

44 We had peaches and cream for our _____.

Make the **sentences** more interesting by adding a **clause** to each of them.

45 My friend knows more about horses than I do.

_____

**46** My Uncle Matt is coming to stay.

**47** We enjoyed the band at the wedding.

**48** Harry swam thirty-six lengths of the school pool.

**49** I love going out on my bike.

**50** This year we are going on holiday to France.

Write the modern version of each of the following words.

**51** hath _____  **52** shouldst _____

**53** cometh _____  **54** hither _____

**55** art _____  **56** wilt _____

**57** saith _____  **58** shalt _____

Add the missing apostrophes.

**59** the cats tail  **60** the five childrens coats

**61** the apples pips  **62** the three dogs bones

**63** the seven houses keys  **64** the videos case

**65** the four horses foals  **66** the six computers keyboards

Add the missing **collective nouns**.

67  A _____ of cattle.

68  A _____ of insects.

69  A _____ of lions.

70  A _____ of musicians.

71  A _____ of puppies.

72  A _____ of sheep.

73  A _____ of crows.

Add the **suffix** *ship* or *ment* to each of these words.

74–81   engage    align    member    receiver    censor

scholar    enhance    content

_____   _____   _____

_____   _____   _____

_____   _____

Rewrite the passage, separating the words correctly and adding the missing capital letters and punctuation.

82–96  itwassundayafternoonthesunwasglintingthroughthetreesanditwaswarm ameliacalledtogeorgearewegoingtodosomethingtodayi'mboredofjustsitting hereheignoredher

_____

_____

_____

_____

_____

_____

Make up your own **mnemonic** for each of these words.

97 weight _____

98 concentration _____

99 permanent _____

100 unfortunately _____

*Now go to the Progress Chart to record your score!* Total ◯ 100

# Paper 10

### Victoria (r. 1837–1901)

*Queen Victoria maintained a detailed diary, her famous Journal, which is contained in 111 large manuscript volumes. These volumes constitute about a third of the original, as her diaries were edited after her death by her youngest daughter Princess Beatrice, at Queen Victoria's request.*

**On William IV's death, and her accession aged 18 years: Tuesday, 20 June 1837 at Kensington Palace**

I was awoke at 6 o'clock by Mamma, who told me that the Archbishop of Canterbury and Lord Conyngham were here, and wished to see me. I got out of bed and went into my sitting-room (only in my dressing-gown), and *alone*, and saw them. Lord Conyngham (the Lord Chamberlain) then acquainted me that my poor Uncle, the King, was no more, and had expired at 12 minutes past 2 this morning, and consequently that I am *Queen*. Lord Conyngham knelt down and kissed my hand, at the same time delivering to me the official announcement of the poor King's demise. The Archbishop then told me that the Queen was desirous that he should come and tell me the details of the last moments of my poor, good Uncle; he said that he had directed his mind to religion, and had died in a perfectly happy, quiet state of mind, and was quite prepared for his death. He added that the King's sufferings at the last were not very great but that there was a good deal of uneasiness. Lord Conyngham, whom I charged to express my feelings of condolence and sorrow to the poor Queen, returned directly to Windsor. I then went to my room and dressed.

    Since it has pleased Providence to place me in this station, I shall do my utmost to fulfil my duty towards my country; I am very young and perhaps in many, though not in all things, inexperienced, but I am sure, that very few have more real good will and more real desire to do what is fit and right than I have ...

At 9 came Lord Melbourne, whom I saw in my room, and of COURSE *quite* ALONE as I shall *always* do all my Ministers. He kissed my hand and I then acquainted him that it had long been my intention to retain him and the rest of the present Ministry at the head of affairs, and that it could not be in better hands than his ... He then read to me the Declaration which I was to read to the Council, which he wrote himself and which is a very fine one. I then talked with him some little longer time after which he left me ... I like him very much and feel confidence in him. He is a very straightforward, honest, clever and good man. I then wrote a letter to the Queen ...

**Coronation: Thursday, 28 June 1838**

I was awoke at four o'clock by the guns in the Park, and could not get much sleep afterwards on account of the noise of the people, bands, etc. Got up at 7 feeling strong and well; the Park presented a curious spectacle; crowds of people up to Constitution Hill, soldiers, bands, etc. I dressed, having taken a little breakfast before I dressed, and a little after. At half past 9 I went into the next room dressed exactly in my House of Lords costume ... At 10 I got into the State Coach with the Duchess of Sutherland and Lord Albemarle, and we began our progress.

It was a fine day, and the crowds of people exceeded what I have ever seen; many as there were the day I went to the City, it was nothing – nothing to the multitudes, the millions of my loyal subjects who were assembled in *every* spot to witness the Procession. Their good humour and excessive loyalty was beyond everything, and I really cannot say *how* proud I feel to be the Queen of *such* a *Nation*. I was alarmed at times for fear that the people would be crushed and squeezed on account of the tremendous rush and pressure.

I reached the Abbey (Westminster) amid deafening cheers at a little after half past 11; I first went into a robing-room quite close to the entrance, where I found my eight Train-bearers – all dressed alike and beautifully, in white satin and silver tissue, with wreaths of silver corn-ears in front, and a small one of pink roses round the plait behind, and pink roses in the trimming of the dresses. After putting on my Mantle, and the young ladies having properly got hold of it, and Lord Conyngham holding the end of it, I left the robing-room and the Procession began. The sight was splendid; the bank of Peeresses quite beautiful, all in their robes, and the Peers on the other side. My young Train-bearers were always near me, and helped whenever I wanted anything. The Bishop of Durham stood on one side near me.

At the beginning of the Anthem ... I retired to St Edward's Chapel, a small dark place immediately behind the Altar, with my Ladies and Train-bearers; took off my crimson robe and kirtle and put on the Supertunica of Cloth of Gold, also in the shape of a kirtle, which was put over a singular sort of little gown of linen trimmed with lace; I also took off my circlet of diamonds, and then proceeded bare-headed into the Abbey; I was then seated upon St Edward's chair where the Dalmatic robe was clasped round me by the Lord Great Chamberlain. Then followed all the various things; and last (of those things) the Crown being placed on my head; – which was, I must own, a most beautiful impressive moment; *all* the Peers and Peeresses put on their Coronets at the same instant ... The shouts, which were very great, the drums, the trumpets, the firing of the guns, all at the same instant, rendered the spectacle most imposing.

... the Procession being formed, I replaced my Crown (which I had taken off for a few minutes), took the Orb in my left hand and the Sceptre in my right, and thus *loaded* proceeded through the Abbey, which resounded with cheers … At about half past 4 I re-entered my carriage, the Crown on my head and Sceptre and Orb in my hand, and we proceeded the same way as we came – the crowds if possible having increased. The enthusiasm, affection and loyalty was really touching, and I shall ever remember this day as the proudest of my life. I came home at a little after 6, – really *not* feeling tired. 70

… I then sat on the sofa for a little while … Mamma … remained to see the Illuminations, and only came in later … I said to Lord Melbourne when I first sat down, I felt a little tired on my feet … Spoke of the weight of the robes etc. and he turned round to me and said *so* kindly, 'And you did it beautifully, – every part of it, with so much taste; it's a thing that you can't give a person advice upon; it must be left to a person.' … Stayed in the drawing-room till 20 minutes past 11, but remained till 12 o'clock on Mamma's balcony looking at the fireworks in Green Park, which were quite beautiful. 75

80

From The British Monarchy web site *[http://www.royal.gov.uk]*

Answer these questions.

1  Who edited Queen Victoria's diaries after her death?

2  Where did Victoria hear of the King's death?

3  What relation was the King to Victoria? _____

4–5  Give the meaning of the following words as they are used in the extracts:

desirous (line 8) _____

condolence (line 14) _____

6–7  Describe in your own words Victoria's first thoughts on becoming Queen.

8–9  Victoria wrote a letter to the Queen. What do you think she might have included in it? Use evidence from the extract to support your answer.

10  How long after hearing about the King's death was Victoria crowned?

**11–12** Victoria awoke at four o'clock on the morning of her Coronation. She states she 'could not get much sleep afterwards on account of the noise of the people, bands, etc.'. What else do you think might have kept her awake?

_____

_____

**13** Why, on lines 58–59, did Victoria proceed 'bare-headed into the Abbey'?

_____

**14** Why do you think the young Queen Victoria described herself as '*loaded*', on line 68?

_____

**15** In addition to the Crown, name one other object that was given to the new Queen during the ceremony.

_____

**16–17** Give two reasons why so many people gathered to watch the Queen go by.

_____

_____

**18–20** Using evidence from the diary extracts, describe in your own words how Victoria felt at her Coronation.

_____

_____

_____

Underline the word on each line which has the same meaning as the word in bold, and ring the word which has the opposite meaning.

| | | | | | |
|---|---|---|---|---|---|
| **21–22 blame** | wrong | careless | censure | bad | praise |
| **23–24 elevate** | high | raise | lower | elude | bottom |
| **25–26 assemble** | disperse | divide | together | unite | gather |
| **27–28 expand** | larger | contract | smaller | increase | disband |
| **29–30 least** | little | most | minimum | lot | more |

Add a different **conjunction** to complete each **sentence**.

31  I intend to go _____ you like it or not.

32  We had to wait in the rain _____ the bus came.

33  You won't finish your drawing _____ you hurry up.

34  You must make the cake _____ it is your party.

Each of these words has a missing silent letter. Rewrite each word with its missing letter.

35  rythm  _____

36  rein  _____

37  not  _____

38  rombus  _____

39  colum  _____

40  our  _____

41  hym  _____

42  gard  _____

State whether each of these sentences has an **active** or **passive** verb.

43  The dog eats his bone.  _____

44  The ice-cream will be eaten by Grandad.  _____

45  Jess swam thirty lengths of the pool.  _____

46  The car crashed into the lamp post.  _____

47  Rudi caught the thief.  _____

48  The bill will be paid by Uncle Rick.  _____

49  Alice was taken to the cinema by her parents.  _____

Match each word with its **definition** in bold by writing the correct number in the space.

(1) **hermit**   (2) **moisture**   (3) **frighten**   (4) **nearby**
(5) **dregs**   (6) **sitting**   (7) **enemy**   (8) **responsible**

50  intimidate  ___

51  sedentary  ___

52  sediment  ___

53  humidity  ___

54  adversary  ___

55  liable  ___

56  recluse  ___

57  adjacent  ___

Write a statement and a question that include the words in bold.

**58–59 Peter   homework**

Statement _____

Question _____

**60–61 sailing   France   holiday**

Statement _____

Question _____

**62–63 photograph   class   yesterday**

Statement _____

Question _____

**64–65 chickenpox   bed   infectious**

Statement _____

Question _____

Write what you think each **prefix** means and then write a word with each **prefix**.

e.g. **bi** =       two              bicycle

**66–67 tele** = _____    _____

**68–69 micro** = _____    _____

**70–71 sub** = _____    _____

**72–73 aqua** = _____    _____

**74–75 auto** = _____    _____

Underline the **prepositions** in the following **sentences**.

76  His book is different from mine.

77  Mrs Trueman is an authority on beetles.

78  That is an exception to the rule.

79  They were not allowed beyond the fence.

80  The drink spilt on the table.

81  Susie saw the strange man outside her window.

82  The fireman raced up the ladder to save the child.

Write four sentences, each with a colon. In two of the sentences use the colon to introduce a quotation and in the other two to introduce a list.

83 _____

84 _____

85 _____

86 _____

Write the simple **past tense** of these **verbs**.

87 to fight _____  88 to build _____

89 to run _____  90 to get _____

91 to mean _____  92 to become _____

93 to find _____  94 to feel _____

Rewrite these words correctly.

95 intresting _____  96 unfortuntely _____

97 specfication _____  98 infrstructure _____

99 rehersal _____  100 indepndence _____

*Now go to the Progress Chart to record your score!*   Total ◯ 100

# Progress Chart — English 11⁺-12⁺ years Book 1

| Total marks | Paper 1 | 2 | 3 | 4 | 5 | 6 | 7 | 8 | 9 | 10 | Percentage |
|---|---|---|---|---|---|---|---|---|---|---|---|
| 100 | | | | | | | | | | | 100% |
| 90 | | | | | | | | | | | 90% |
| | | | | | | | | | | | 85% |
| 80 | | | | | | | | | | | 80% |
| 70 | | | | | | | | | | | 70% |
| 60 | | | | | | | | | | | 60% |
| 50 | | | | | | | | | | | 50% |
| 40 | | | | | | | | | | | 40% |
| 30 | | | | | | | | | | | 30% |
| 20 | | | | | | | | | | | 20% |
| 10 | | | | | | | | | | | 10% |
| 0 | 1 | 2 | 3 | 4 | 5 | 6 | 7 | 8 | 9 | 10 | 0% |

Date

*When you've finished the book use the Next Step Planner* →